THE PERSON...

HOLINESS

The Blessings
of the
Good Life

LARRY RICHARDS

THOMAS NELSON PUBLISHERS
Nashville • Atlanta • London • Vancouver

CONTENTS

PREFACE . . . . *iv*

SpiritBuilding
Growing Toward Total Wholeness

CHAPTER 1: Good News for Imperfect People *1*

FaithBuilding
Growing Closer to God

CHAPTER 2: Holy, Holy, Holy *9*
CHAPTER 3: Inside Out *17*
CHAPTER 4: No Other Gods *25*
CHAPTER 5: No Likeness of Anything *33*
CHAPTER 6: Taking God's Name in Vain *41*
CHAPTER 7: Remember the Sabbath *49*

RelationshipBuilding
Growing Wiser in Living with Others

CHAPTER 8: Honor Parents *57*

CharacterBuilding
Growing Strong from the Inside Out

CHAPTER 9: You Shall Not Murder *65*

RelationshipBuilding
Growing Wiser in Living with Others

CHAPTER 10: You Shall Not Commit Adultery *73*

CharacterBuilding
Growing Strong from the Inside Out

CHAPTER 11: You Shall Not Steal *81*
CHAPTER 12: You Shall Not Bear False Witness *89*
CHAPTER 13: You Shall Not Covet *97*
TEACHING PLAN *105*

PREFACE

What is Personal Growth?

The idea behind the **Personal Growth**™ **Study Guide** series of books is that we grow in three dimensions. We grow internally (CharacterBuilding). We grow in and through our relationship with God (FaithBuilding). And we grow in and through our relationship with others (RelationshipBuilding).

Each **Personal Growth**™ **Study Guide** book explores a significant aspect of human life in terms of character building, faith building, and relationship building. The first four books, available now in your Christian bookstore or from the publisher, explore Intimacy, Holiness, Fulfillment, and Forgiveness. Look for additional titles, coming soon.

There is also a **Personal Growth**™ **Study Bible.** This vital study and devotional Bible identifies and comments on key passages throughout God's Word that help us develop Christian character, Christian faith, and Christian interpersonal relationships. The quotes at the end of the chapters are insights taken from the **Personal Growth**™ **Study Bible.**

If you want to build your life on God's Word, don't miss getting this practical and invaluable Bible, available NOW.

Personal Growth™ Study Guide Books

Personal Growth™ **Study Guide** books are topical. They provide in-depth insights into life's most significant issues. Their focus is illustrated by these first four compelling titles:

Intimacy: The secrets of loving and being loved
Forgiveness: The gift that heals and sets free
Holiness: The blessings of the good life
Fulfillment: The adventure of life worth living

Personal Growth™ **Study Guide** books are rooted in Scripture and grow out of the author's conviction that God's Word supplies all the guidance we need. These fresh, easy-to-read books provide easy access to biblical principles that can revolutionize our lives.

How to Use Personal Growth™ Study Guide Books

Personal Growth™ **Study Guide** books are written for your personal enrichment. One way to use these books is to read them in your own home. Questions at the end of each chapter will help you apply principles to your life, while quotes from the **Personal Growth**™ **Study Bible** encourage meditation.

Personal Growth™ **Study Guide** books are also ideal for study groups. There's a Teaching Plan section at the back of each book designed to stimulate shared exploration of the life-changing truths developed in each chapter. **Personal Growth**™ **Study Guide** book studies can add a dynamic dimension to your Sunday school class, home Bible study, vacation Bible school, or other group meetings. While the **Personal Growth**™ **Study Guides** were designed with the **Personal Growth**™ **Study Bible** in mind, you may use them with any Bible and get full benefit from them!

The NEW Personal Growth™ Study Bible

Personal Growth™ **Study Guide** books are intimately linked to the new **Personal Growth**™ **Study Bible.** Each book develops in a single study one of the many essential Personal Growth themes identified in the study Bible. This unique study Bible explores the whole Word of God, highlights principles that will help believers understand how to grow in a personal relationship with God and relationships with others, and shows how to develop a strong, godly character. Unlike other study Bibles, which concentrate on providing information about the text, the **Personal Growth**™ **Study Bible** concentrates on identifying the Personal Growth principles in Scripture and applying these principles daily. The **Personal Growth**™ **Study Bible** points to key texts and how to understand them, and then leads to God's goal of transformation!

About the Author

The **Personal Growth**™ **Study bible** and **Personal Growth**™ **Study Guide** books are the work of Dr. Larry Richards. Larry has written over 140 books in his 30-year ministry. His works include Christian Education textbooks which have been translated into 22 languages and are used in leading Bible colleges and seminaries throughout the world. Larry is the author of *The Expository Dictionary of Bible Words*, which explores the Greek and Hebrew roots of Scripture, *The Revell Bible Dictionary*, and many other works on Scripture.

Most important to Larry are the many devotional and study books he's written which speak to the hearts of believers. The **Personal Growth**™ **Study Bible** and **Personal Growth**™ **Study Guide** books are the culmination of Larry's thirty years of studying and teaching God's Word.

GOOD NEWS FOR IMPERFECT PEOPLE

*B*ob remembers his mother as a stern, quiet woman, who awed both him and his father with her aura of holiness. Mother prayed long prayers at the table. Mother always moved slowly, deliberately, an austere figure who dominated the household. Mother never lost her temper. But both Bob and his dad lived in dread of her look of disdain, of her slightly curled lip as she turned her head to stare at them unblinkingly. The look alone was enough to make Bob feel guilty, whether or not he knew what he'd done to earn her disapproval. The look alone was enough to drive Bob's dad to the barn, where he puttered with the farm machinery until it got so late he had to return to the house. Bob never talked with his dad about how he felt, but very early sensed that he and his father failed to meet the high standards expected by his mother and, of course, by God. Bob always thought of his mother, who died before he reached his teens, as a truly holy woman. Compared to her, he and his dad weren't holy at all.

Years later, when Bob was the dynamic pastor of a successful, growing church, those childhood feelings kept sweeping back. Others respected him and his obvious passion for the ministry. But within, Bob was torn and miserable. How many Saturday nights he had spent on his knees at the altar in the church sanctuary, agonizing over his failure to love God perfectly! How many Saturday nights he seemed to sense God, staring at him with his mother's unblinking gaze, aware of faults that Bob himself could hardly imagine. Whatever Bob did, however hard he worked, however enthusiastically others responded to his ministry, deep down Bob knew that it wasn't enough. He was deeply aware that he was an imperfect person trapped in the service of a God who demands perfection.

Harry Ironside, who ministered two generations ago, told the story of his own agonizing search for perfection. At one time he lived in a denominational boarding house. There he met a young woman whose quiet piety Harry deeply admired. She seemed so serene. So at peace. Everything about her demeanor spoke of a holiness that Ironside desperately yearned for. After several weeks he determined to confront her and demand to know her secret. One night as he gathered his courage and was about to go see her, there was a knock on the door of his room.

It was the young woman he so admired. As soon as he opened the door, the young woman blurted out, with tears in her eyes, "I've got to know! You've got to tell me. What is the secret of holiness?"

The Secret of Holiness

When we look at the Bible we're struck by statements the New Testament makes about perfection and holiness.

One of the strongest statements was made by Jesus Himself as He called on listeners to love their enemies. "You shall be perfect," Jesus said, "as your Father in heaven is perfect" (Matt. 5:48). This alone would be enough to establish the standard. But there is more. In Ephesians 4:13 the apostle speaks of the Christian community coming to the knowledge of God's Son, "to a perfect man, to the measure of the stature of the fullness of Christ." In Colossians 1:28 Paul says that the goal of his ministry is to "present every man perfect in Christ Jesus." Later he speaks of prayers "that you may stand perfect and complete in all the will of God" (Col. 4:12). Add the testimony of James 1:4, encouraging patience "that you may be perfect and complete, lacking nothing," and we can't help but be convinced that God really does expect perfection from us.

What is the secret of holiness?

It's even more clear as we look at New Testament passages on holiness. Paul urges believers to present their bodies to God as a living sacrifice, "holy, acceptable to God, which is your reasonable service" (Rom. 12:1). Ephesians 1:4 reminds us that God chose believers "in Him before the foundation of the world, that we should be holy and without blame before Him." Colossians 3:12 explains that "as the elect of God, holy and beloved," we're to live a distinctive kind of life.

Most familiar, and most challenging, are verses in 1 Peter:

But as He who called you is holy, you also be holy in all your conduct, because it is written, *"Be holy, for I am holy."*
1 Peter 1:15, 16

You also, as living stones, are being built up into a spiritual house, a holy priesthood.   *1 Peter 2:5*

But you are a chosen generation, a royal priesthood, a holy nation, His own special people.   *1 Peter 2:9*

His Own Special People

That was what bothered both Bob and Harry Ironside. They knew that as Christians they were God's own special people. Each wanted to *be* special. Each yearned to be perfect. Each wanted desperately to be holy. But each was deeply aware that, however he appeared to others, he was not perfect. Neither was the truly holy person he yearned to be.

Not everyone feels the same sense of urgency about holiness. Many of us Christians are relatively satisfied with our lives. We're "good people." We love our spouses and are faithful. We invest in our children and chauffeur them to all those activities. We guide their studies. We try to be good neighbors. We go to church regularly. Often we give our time generously to teach Sunday school or serve on some board or committee. We give an honest day's work on our job, and we try to get along with our coworkers. We're careful of our language and are certainly uncomfortable when people curse and swear or tell off-color jokes in our presence. We obey the law, except maybe for speeding just a little. We're good citizens and vote regularly. In short, we live a pretty good life. We know we're not perfect, but we're generally comfortable with ourselves.

The chances are that it's only now and then, when tweaked by a twinge of guilt over something we've done or haven't done, that we feel less than comfortable with ourselves and with our faith. After all, what does God expect? Perfection?

If we should suddenly decide to take seriously the idea that as God's special people we are to be *truly* different, we

Christians are God's own special people.

might begin to feel a bit more like Bob and Harry Ironside. What if we should decide to take seriously a verse that says "but as He who called you is holy, you also be holy" (1 Pet. 1:15)? Then we'd probably be a little less comfortable with ourselves and with our lives.

The problem is, of course, that we *are* God's special people. As a people purchased at the awesome cost of Christ's lifeblood, we *are* called to be perfect. As God's representatives in this world, we *are* to be holy and shine as lights in the darkness. Bob and Harry, whatever the genesis of their deep concern with holiness, were right to yearn to be all they could be. Bob and Harry, whatever the torment misunderstanding holiness and perfection caused, were closer to the heart of God than are comfortable Christians who assume that it's enough for God's special people to be *nice* people rather than strive for holiness.

Striving for Holiness

The problem experienced by Bob and Harry and by thousands of other Christians striving for holiness is that they seem to make no progress *achieving* holiness. At least, neither *felt* he was achieving holiness. That sense of failure was rooted in part in each one's idea of what it would be like to be perfect; what it would be like to be truly holy.

Check the following clusters of statements. Which option under each cluster do *you* think best represents the holiness that God expects of His special people?

Holiness Checklist

A. In my relationship with my spouse, holiness is:
    ___ 1. Not feeling anything for him/her but selfless love.
    ___ 2. Not expressing any feelings except positive, loving feelings.
    ___ 3. Not acting intentionally or unintentionally in any way that might hurt him/her.
    ___ 4. Acting intentionally with his/her interests in mind.

B. In my relationship with God, holiness is:
    ___ 1. Constantly being in a state of praising and loving God.

___ 2. Constantly being aware that I am in the center of God's will.

___ 3. Committing myself to daily Bible reading, prayer, church-going, and witnessing.

___ 4. Seeking to live each day in a way that pleases and honors the Lord.

C. In my relationship with work and coworkers, holiness is:

___ 1. Never failing to display God's perfection in the way I do my work.

___ 2. Never failing to speak out against sin and encouraging others to accept God's forgiveness.

___ 3. Never speaking or acting out of character as one of God's people.

___ 4. Giving my best to my work and showing love to my coworkers.

D. In my thought life, holiness is:

___ 1. Never having a hostile or unclean thought.

___ 2. Never exposing myself to any TV or other media which contains violence or makes sexual references.

___ 3. Never expressing any hostile or unclean thoughts I have.

___ 4. Consciously choosing to think about the good, the true, and the beautiful.

E. In regard to sins, holiness is:

___ 1. Being completely free of sinful thoughts and deeds.

___ 2. Never committing any kind of sin at all.

___ 3. Never committing any intentional sins.

___ 4. Being sensitive to sins and confessing them to the Lord.

One problem for both Bob and Harry was that each defined holiness in terms of option 1. They believed that a truly holy person would never feel anything but selfless love for his or her spouse. A truly holy person would constantly be in a state of praising and loving God. A truly holy person would never fail to display God's own perfection in the way he or she works. A truly holy person would never have a hostile or unclean thought. And a truly holy person would be completely free of sinful thoughts and deeds.

The problem with this view of holiness is that only One person ever achieved it, Jesus Himself! And while we are to grow more and more like Jesus in our essential character, unlike Jesus we have a sinful nature that makes the kind of perfection Bob and Harry expected of themselves impossible!

That's why the apostle John, writing in his first epistle, says, "If we walk in the light as He is in the light, we have fellowship with one another, and the blood of Jesus Christ His Son cleanses us from all sin" (1:7). Our first impression is that walking in the light must refer to utter holiness: to complete sinlessness. But John says that if we are walking in the light, Christ's blood "cleanses us from all sin." If walking in the light were sinlessness, surely we'd have no need to be cleansed from sins!

The passage goes on to underline this truth. John writes, "if we say we have no sin, we deceive ourselves, and the truth is not in us" (1:8). Whatever the perfection and holiness that Scripture calls us to as God's special people, it is not a state where we can claim we "have no sin." In fact, the notion that we have reached the place where we have no sin is something Scripture labels self deceit!

Oh, it's nice to be able to dismiss an outburst of anger as a holy expression of "righteous indignation." Or to disguise gossip as a request for prayer. It may have seemed nice to Bob's mother to avoid dealing with the cold and judgmental attitude she projected by acting as if she were holier than her husband and son. But as John teaches, if we say, even to ourselves, that "we have no sin," then "the truth is not in us."

What God expects is that we will be honest with ourselves about our faults and failures. We are to walk in the light, not trying to hide our flaws by drawing a theological cloak of denial over them. We are to walk in the light, and when we sin, we are to "confess our sins." When we do, God "is faithful and just to forgive us our sins."

The last phrase in this verse is particularly important. God not only forgives. When we are honest with ourselves and with Him and acknowledge our sins, God continues His cleansing work within us.

Holy Sinners

It seems like such a paradox. We Christians aren't to claim there is no sin in us. We are to accept the fact that at heart we are sinners, and that we sin now and will sin in the future. Yet we Christians are also called to be perfect. We are called to be holy, as God is Holy.

As strange as it seems, the Bible portrays Christians as holy sinners!

Part of our problem with holiness lies in the fact that we tend to misunderstand what the words "perfect" and "holy" mean. And part of our problem lies in the fact that we fail to take seriously the Bible's affirmation that we are sinners.

Uncomfortable sinners like Bob and Harry Ironside, who are totally committed to serving the Lord, torment themselves when they fall short because they misunderstand how the words "perfect" and "holy" are applied to God's people. Comfortable sinners, surely the majority these days, miss out because they fail to realize that God truly expects them to live a life of uncompromising commitment. We are not to settle for being "nice" people, but are to make it our goal to be perfect and holy.

That's why the study we're undertaking in this book can be so important. An understanding of true holiness can release those who, like Bob, struggle to live up to unrealistic expectations. And an understanding of true holiness can bring excitement into the life of the "comfortable" Christian who has never realized that Christianity promises a dynamic daily adventure in close company with our Lord.

FOR REFLECTION

1. Do you see yourself as more like Bob, or more the "comfortable Christian"? In what way(s)?

_____

_____

_____

2. Which options in the A through E statements on pages 4 and 5 did you check? What do your answers suggest about your idea of holiness?

_____

_____

_____

3. Just for fun, write out one paragraph in which you describe a "holy person."

_____

_____

_____

Before going on to the next chapter, meditate for a time on the following article on 1 Peter 2:9, 10 from the Personal Growth™ Study Bible.

Just be yourself. These are freeing words as long as we feel good about ourselves. But if we feel weak, or lacking in ability, "be yourself" doesn't help at all.

What might God have in mind if He were to say, "Just be yourself"? Would He be thinking of us as sinners? No, according to 1 Peter 2:9, God sees us as a chosen generation. He sees us as a royal priesthood. As citizens of a holy nation. He sees each of us as His own special possession. And as His people, we are special indeed.

It's a well-known fact that people tend to act in accord with their image of themselves. If we see ourselves as inadequate, we don't even try. However beautiful a person may be, if she doesn't feel beautiful she won't act as if she were beautiful.

God wants us to understand our identity in Christ that we might act in accord with who we really are. Not in accord with who we once were.

HOLY, HOLY, HOLY

*O*ne of the most dramatic scenes in Scripture is sketched for us in Isaiah 6. The young Isaiah has a vision of the Lord in the Jerusalem temple. God is seated on a throne. Hovering in the air above the throne, and sheltering it with one of three sets of giant wings, are angels called seraphim. When one cries to another,

> Holy, holy, holy is the LORD of hosts;
> The whole earth is full of His glory!
> *Isaiah 6:3*

the temple is shaken, and smoke fills the room.

Isaiah is terrified. Whatever else can be said of this apparition, this Holy God is wholly other. Isaiah is suddenly overwhelmed with an awareness of his own sinfulness. He crumples to the floor and cries out in despair:

> Woe is me, for I am undone!
> Because I am a man of unclean lips,
> And I dwell in the midst of a
>   people of unclean lips;
> For my eyes have seen the King,
> The LORD of hosts.
> *Isaiah 6:5*

Isaiah's emotions remind us of Bob, the pastor we met in the last chapter. The more Bob struggled to be perfect, the more he yearned to live a perfect Christian life, the more troubled he became. His awareness of God's concern with holiness drove him to despair. Instead of finding peace and fulfillment in his search for holiness Bob, like Isaiah, found himself crying out, "Woe is me."

The Second "Holy"

It is certainly true that the realm of the holy is awesome. It is the realm inhabited by God Himself, and human beings who become aware of what God is like in His essential Being are struck with a sense of their own sinfulness.

Yet the Old Testament frequently speaks of God as Israel's Holy One with an entirely different association.

Psalm 22:3, 4 says "You are holy, enthroned in the praises of Israel. Our fathers trusted in You; they trusted, and You delivered them."

Psalm 78:41, 42 says "Yes, again and again they tempted God, and limited the Holy One of Israel. They did not remember His power; the day when He redeemed them from the enemy."

Psalm 89 celebrates God as Creator, and One whose rule is founded on righteousness and justice, whose character is the source of mercy and truth. The psalmist takes comfort in the fact that "our shield belongs to the LORD, and our king to the Holy One of Israel" (89:18).

The sense of celebration is also seen in Isaiah 12, where the prophet looks ahead to a day of redemption.

> And in that day you will say:
> "O LORD, I will praise You;
> Though You were angry with me,
> Your anger is turned away, and You comfort
>   me.
> Behold, God is my salvation;
> I will trust and not be afraid;
> 'For Yah, the LORD, is my strength and song;
> He also has become my salvation.'"
>
> "Cry out and shout, O inhabitant of Zion,
> For great is the Holy One of Israel
>   in your midst."
>
> *Isaiah 12:1, 2, 6*

While the image of God as Holy remains awesome, these writers of Scripture do not find the Holy One frightening.

Indeed, God's holiness is linked with deliverance (Ps. 21), redemption from enemies (Ps. 78), and shielding Israel from danger (Ps. 89:18). Even after experiencing terrible national discipline, Isaiah proclaims a day when God's anger will be turned away. God will comfort and save, and God's people will shout for the joy of having the Holy One of Israel among them.

These writers of Scripture do not find the Holy One frightening.

These promises mirror Isaiah's experience. His initial reaction to the vision of God as Israel's Holy One was an overwhelming sense of his own sinfulness. God as Holy *is* wholly other. We are not like Him in His perfection. We are not like Him in His utter, uncompromising righteousness. And so, sensing the terrible gap, we cry "I am undone! Because I am a man of unclean lips," (Is. 6:5). We are sinners and members of a sinful race, separated by our condition from a God who is utterly holy in His nature and character.

But if we return to the story of Isaiah's vision of the Lord we make a fascinating discovery. Isaiah is repelled by his sinfulness. But God is not!

One of the seraphim takes a live coal from the altar of sacrifice and flies with it to Isaiah. He touches the coal to Isaiah's lips, and announces:

> Behold, this has touched your lips;
> Your iniquity is taken away.
> And your sin is purged.
>
> *Isaiah 6:7*

Forgiveness, purchased at the altar of sacrifice, has cleansed Isaiah. As a forgiven sinner Isaiah can now stand, secure, in the very presence of Israel's Holy God!

But there's even more. Isaiah hears God's voice asking "Whom shall I send, and who will go for Us?" Isaiah, filled with gratitude and joy, responds immediately. "Here am I! Send me!"

And God says, "Go" (Is. 6:8, 9).

What a transformation!

At first Isaiah is crushed in the presence of the Holy God. Isaiah is overwhelmed by a sense of his own sinfulness and unworthiness. But then God acts to forgive and to cleanse. Isaiah is now overwhelmed with another emotion entirely, an emotion often reflected in the psalms quoted above. As a redeemed and forgiven person Isaiah is filled with gratitude, joy, and praise. And when God asks whom He can send, Isaiah can't wait to volunteer!

It is appropriate for us as forgiven sinners to experience joy and gratitude, and out of gratitude to serve Him all our lives.

Each of these reactions is an appropriate response to God's holiness.

It is appropriate for us to feel despair as we sense our own sinfulness. Bob and Harry Ironside were right to despair as they attempted as sinners to match the holiness of a holy God.

But it is also appropriate for us to feel relief as we realize that God's holiness has motivated Him to provide the forgiveness and cleansing we so desperately need. We stand before God as *forgiven* sinners, and because of this we have the confidence we need to approach His throne boldly.

And it is appropriate for us as forgiven sinners to experience joy and gratitude, and out of gratitude to volunteer gladly to serve Him all our lives.

Revisiting Bob

Bob's experience with his mother led him to imagine a one-dimensional holiness. His mother's cold disapproval and her obvious rejection led Bob to feel his sinfulness deeply. He struggled to please her but felt that he could never measure up to her high standards. After his mother died, Bob's impression of his mother shaped his view of God. Whenever Bob thought of God as holy, he seemed to sense his mother's disapproving stare. He saw her mouth curled downward, full of contempt for his futile efforts truly to be and do good.

Perhaps someone has had the same kind of impact on your life and given you a similar one-dimensional impression of

God. You're like Isaiah, overwhelmed with guilt at being in the presence of a Holy God. Try as you will, you can't be satisfied with your best efforts to please Him, and you remain constantly aware that you fall short daily.

The good news for you in Scripture is that while your response to God as Holy has been appropriate, it has been one-dimensional. You've failed to go beyond Isaiah's initial experience. You've failed to see that in Christ God has taken a burning coal from eternity's altar. He has touched your lips and, as you have put your faith in Jesus, God has announced:

> Behold, this has touched *your* lips;
> *Your* iniquity is taken away.
> And *your* sin is purged.
>
> *Isaiah 6:7*

Our Holy God does not intend you to spend the rest of your life carrying the burden of your sins. Our Holy God *lifts that burden from us!* Our Holy God cleanses and forgives. And we rejoice!

But that's not all! When the full awareness of God's great gift fills our hearts, we respond by committing ourselves to Him! "Who will go for Us?" "Why, I will! You have lifted the burden of my sin. You have set me on my feet in Your Holy presence. Now how gladly my life I give, henceforth to live, Oh Christ for you alone."

"Holy, Holy, Holy."

How appropriate that this word is repeated three times. And how important, as we begin to think about holiness, that we keep each dimension of God's holiness in clear view.

"Holy"—Lord, I am overwhelmed by a sense of my sinfulness!

"Holy"—Lord, You forgive and cleanse me!

"Holy"—Lord, from now on I set myself apart to live for You!

Set Apart for God

If we look at the Old Testament word for "holy" we discover that the verb means "to be consecrated" or "to be dedicated." *The Expository Dictionary of Bible Words* says that "anything which is 'holy' is set apart. It is removed from the realm of the common and moved to the sphere of the sacred."[1]

In most instances in the Old Testament "holy" is a technical religious term used to describe persons, places, times, and objects that are considered sacred because they are consecrated to God. The Sabbath is called holy (Ex. 20:8–11). Israel's priests are called holy (Lev. 21:7). Mount Sinai, where God appeared to give the Ten Commandments, is called holy (Ex. 19:23). Israel itself is called holy, for the entire nation was chosen by God to be His own possession (Deut. 7:6).

The early books of the Old Testament emphasize ritual holiness. For instance, vessels used in the temple could not be used for any other purpose. Rules concerning diet and clothing and other aspects of Israel's daily life were carefully regulated, and a person who violated these regulations was considered ritually "unclean." He was no longer "holy," in the sense that he was no longer fit for service or to worship God until the uncleanness was cleansed by another ritual. With the state of ritual cleanness or holiness restored, the Old Testament believer could once again serve Israel's God.

While most Old Testament references to holiness relate to ritual cleanness or uncleanness, there is also a moral component to the concept of personal holiness. Again quoting *The Expository Dictionary of Bible Words,*

> Lev. 19:2 displays a moral dimension to God's holiness. "Speak to the entire assembly of Israel," the Lord told Moses, "and say to them, 'Be holy because I, the Lord your God, am holy.'"
>
> The commands that follow this statement are not ritual but are moral in character. They deal with idolatry, theft, lying, fraud, slander, revenge, etc., and include the command to love one's neighbor. These commands are punctuated regularly by the reminder, "I am the Lord."
>
> In this Old Testament passage and many others, God's holiness is directly linked with his own moral character. That holiness is displayed in his moral perfection and faithful commitment to good and in his judgment on those who desert the way of goodness for sin . . . . When

Israel was set apart to God by God's sovereign choice, both the ritual and moral aspects of obedience to God were essential in their life of holiness.[2]

So while God's first "holy" makes us aware of our sinfulness, and His second "holy" frees us from despair by proclaiming forgiveness, the third "holy" is a call to commitment. It is a call to set ourselves apart to God, and out of gratitude to live a life that honors and pleases our God.

Today Bob pastors a church in a small town and writes curriculum material for a major Sunday school publisher. While now and then the old feelings of worthlessness and despair well up, Bob is able to set them aside. He has passed beyond the first "holy." Bob now lives in the realm of the second "holy" as a *forgiven* sinner. Bob now understands the wonder of God's grace. The awe Bob feels is awe at the great love of God, a love which reaches out to enfold him despite his flaws and failures.

Bob also lives in the realm of the third "holy." He seeks daily to live a life that pleases and glorifies God. But that desire to please God is no longer driven by the feeling that he *has to perform* to win God's favor. Instead Bob's desire to please God is driven by gratitude for the grace Bob experiences daily, a sinner who has been—and is being—forgiven and cleansed.

FOR REFLECTION

1. Which of the three "holy's" of Isaiah 6 best describes where you are today in your own Christian life?

___ Holy   ___ awareness of sin   ___ guilt-driven
___ Holy   ___ awareness of forgiveness   ___ comfortable
___ Holy   ___ deep gratitude for cleansing   ___ committed

2. Other Old Testament passages that speak of God as Israel's Holy One emphasize God's judgment of sin. However, in each case judgment is reserved for those who refuse to acknowledge their sin and put their trust in the Lord. If you wish, check the following: Is. 1:4; 5:19, 24; Jer. 50:29.

Before going on to the next chapter, meditate on the following commentary on Exodus 4:10–12, from the Personal Growth™ Study Bible.

"Leave me alone, God." We can understand Moses' feelings of inadequacy. Forty years before Moses was consumed by dreams of delivering Israel. Now 80, having spent the last four decades as a shepherd, Moses has lost his fire. Moses knows now how foolish his dreams were, and has faced his limitations. He has no gift of oratory that will enable him to move others. He stumbles over his words, and struggles to think of the right thing to say. So Moses shakes his head and begs God to find someone else.

Like Moses, we know how inadequate we are. When opportunities to minister come, we remain silent. When asked to teach, or lead a class, we draw back. We know our shortcomings. Find someone else.

But the God who said to Moses "I will be with your mouth and teach you what you shall say" is with us today. The wonder is that our shortcomings *do not* limit God, or limit His ability to use us today. So, God, don't look for someone else. Use me.

———————
1. *The Expository Dictionary of Bible Words* (Grand Rapids, MI: Zondervan, 1991), 339.
2. Ibid., 339–340.

Inside Out

*K*aren comes from a church and family with very clear ideas about holiness. Like many young people, she questions the convictions of Mom and Dad and the congregation she's attended since childhood.

Actually, Karen realizes that there are many positive things about her home and her church. Mom and Dad are always there for her. They're strict, but Karen realizes it is love and concern that lead them to set limits none of her school friends have. She thinks some of their rules are foolish. But because she respects her parents she keeps the rebellious feelings, that sometimes surge, to herself.

Karen sees many positive things in her church. The congregation is made up of people who've been neighbors for years. They've helped each other out. They've stood by each other when troubles came. They've prayed fervently and seen God answer prayers.

Of course, like any group of people, the folks at her church aren't perfect. They have really strict ideas about what a person should and shouldn't do, and they don't hesitate to express their disapproval of anyone who steps out of line. What bothers Karen most are things like music. Contemporary Christian music is out. It's not the words, but the sound. It's too much like secular music. Karen once read that a lot of church people criticized the songs written and played by the early Salvation Army in England. The Army picked up the tunes and style of the music halls in order to appeal to the person on the street. Church people were shocked. But today those gospel songs are old favorites, a staple in the hymnbook used in Karen's church.

When Karen tried to point that out, no one would listen. And she earned the most disapproving of the looks reserved for young people who question the rules the congregation holds so dear.

And there are other rules. No makeup. No jewelry. No dancing. No movies. (It bugged Karen that a lot of the people in church rented those same movies at the video store. If they were wrong in the theater, what made them right in the home?)

Of course there were "do's" on the list as well. Be at church Sunday morning and evening. Show up for prayer meeting. Have daily devotions. Pray for the right spiritual gifts. Be sure to speak the pious jargon of tradition. And there were many other unspoken rules that were just as strict.

While Karen appreciated the many positive qualities of her congregation, she was bothered by what she saw as its irrelevant rules. And she was especially bothered by the notion that she couldn't even express her thoughts or doubts without being immediately put down by adults.

Irrelevant Rules

If Karen had lived in Old Testament times she might have felt the rules Israel was to live by were even more irrelevant.

How about "Among the animals, whatever divides the hoof, having cloven hooves and chewing the cud—that you may eat. Nevertheless these you shall not eat among those that chew the cud or those that have cloven hooves; the camel, because it chews the cud but does not have cloven hooves, is unclean to you" (Lev. 11:3, 4)?

How about "A woman shall not wear anything that pertains to a man, nor shall a man put on a woman's garment" (Deut. 22:5)?

How about "you shall not plow with an ox and a donkey together" (Deut. 22:10)?

How about "you shall not wear a garment of different sorts, such as wool and linen mixed together" (Deut. 22:11)?

How about "you shall not boil a young goat in its mother's milk" (Ex. 23:19)? No one can imagine why this rule is in the Old Testament, but today the Orthodox Jew maintains two sets of dishes, one for milk and one for meats, and never serves both kinds of products at the same meal. After all, someone might inadvertently mix some animal's meat with its mother's milk and violate the command!

While many of the Old Testament's laws governing the Israelite's way of life can be explained as moral or public-health rulings, many others seem totally irrelevant. Why have four tassels on clothing? Why not cut the corners of a man's beard? Why not cut the hair that curls over the front of a man's ear? Why not eat shrimp, ruled out of the Jewish diet because they lack fins and scales? Why, after sex, wash oneself and one's bedding and be "unclean until evening"?

If we take these and the other rules that govern life in ancient Israel one by one, we feel totally frustrated. So many seem to make no sense at all. But if we step back a pace, and look at the big picture, we note something fascinating. The various laws and rulings of the Old Testament touch on all the basic issues of human life. They govern the way Israel dealt with birth and death. They govern the food Israel ate and the clothing Israel wore. The laws govern sexual expression and every other interpersonal relationship. Israel's laws pay attention to the treatment of animals and aliens, to the conduct of war and the maintenance of peace. Israel's laws define sin and provide for sacrifices which bring the blessing of forgiveness. *In essence, Israel's laws establish boundaries that set God's chosen people apart from every other people on earth!*

> The various laws and rulings of the Old Testament touch on all the basic issues of human life.

The rulings of the Old Testament that governed cleanness and uncleanness (i.e., the state of ritual holiness and the state of ritual unholiness) reminded Israel that God was involved in every aspect of the life of His people. And it reminded Israel that, as a people dedicated to God, they truly were to be special. And different.

Boundaries

Old Testament laws of ritual purity established *external boundaries* that kept the obedient Jew in a state of ritual holiness. There's something of this way of thinking expressed in the emphasis of Karen's congregation on its own distinctive do's and don'ts. These Christians want boundaries, too. They want rules that will let them know when they're in a state of holiness and are pleasing to God.

The problem, and one which Karen senses although she does not yet understand, is that today the boundaries God establishes for believers are *internal*, not external!

Jesus' Sermon on the Mount (Matt. 5—7) has been called the "Constitution of Christ's Kingdom." One section of that sermon focuses our attention on the shift in boundaries that Jesus introduced.

The section begins with Jesus' affirmation that He did not come to destroy the Law or the prophets. In fact, not the dotting of an "i" not the crossing of a "t," will pass away until all the old "is accomplished" (NIV). But Jesus did come to "fulfill" the older revelation.

Jesus' first-century listeners would have understood exactly what Christ was saying. Indeed, it was the earnest desire of every rabbi to "fulfill" the Law, for in that day the phrase meant "to give the true and complete meaning" of God's holy Word.

What Jesus was about to do then was give the true and complete meaning of the Law. How eagerly His hearers must have drawn near!

Jesus began by emphasizing the importance of the Commandments (Matt. 6:19). But He warned that to enter the kingdom of heaven required a righteousness greater than that of the scribes and Pharisees, who boasted about faithfully keeping every detail of the Law. Indeed, in their quest for holiness, the Pharisees tried sincerely to keep every ruling developed from the Law by the sages who interpreted it!

> To "fulfill" meant "to give the true and complete meaning" of God's holy Word.

But what is this greater righteousness the Law requires? In a series of illustrations, Jesus explains. Each illustration has the same form.

1. "You have heard that it was said to those of old,"
2. (A statement of Old Testament Law or rabbinic interpretation)

3. "But I say to you"
4. (Jesus' explanation of God's underlying concern, the true and complete meaning of the commandment which "fulfills" it.)

Let's look at just a few.

"You have heard that it was said to those of old, '*You shall not murder,* and whoever murders will be in danger of the judgment.' But I say to you that whoever is angry with his brother without a cause shall be in danger of the judgment" (5:21, 22).

"You have heard that it was said to those of old, 'You shall not commit adultery.' But I say to you that whoever looks at a woman to lust for her has already committed adultery with her in his heart" (5:27, 28).

"Again you have heard that it was said to those of old, 'You shall not swear falsely, but shall perform your oaths to the Lord.' But I say to you, do not swear at all: . . . but let your 'Yes' be 'Yes,' and your 'No' 'No.' For whatever is more than these is from the evil one" (5:33, 37).

What does each of these illustrations have in common? First the pattern, "You have heard it was said to those of old" . . . "But I say." Jesus clearly is reinterpreting—fulfilling— Old Testament commands. Second, in each illustration Jesus *shifts boundaries*. The Old Testament boundaries are external, dealing with behavior. Don't kill. Don't commit adultery. Don't swear an oath and fail to perform it. But Jesus' boundaries are internal, dealing with the heart!

When the Commandment says "Do not murder," the issue which concerns God is the anger that wells up and is expressed not only in the act of murder but in any hostile act! Murder is the extreme expression of anger. But angry words— "you fool!"—flow from the same source!

When the Commandment says "Do not commit adultery," the issue which concerns God is the lust that wells up in our hearts. The source of adultery is the corruption which views a person made in God's image, and thus of ultimate worth and value to Him, as a mere object, a body to be used rather than a person to be valued for himself or herself.

When the Commandment says "keep your vows," the issue which concerns God is basic integrity. A human being is to be so completely trustworthy that his or her "yes" expresses a commitment which surely will be honored.

Old Testament commandments laid down external boundaries within which God's people were to live. Jesus revealed the stunning truth that all along the issues of life have been *internal* rather than *external!* The righteousness sought by the Pharisees through keeping every detail of the external law simply is not enough. The righteousness with which God is concerned is internal and requires a transformation of the human heart. To live as citizens of Jesus' kingdom, hostility must be replaced by love, lust must be replaced by respect and concern for persons of the opposite sex, and the very need for legal contracts and vows must be made irrelevant by a person's utter, unquestionable integrity.

How shocked Jesus' listeners must have been. They supposed that if they did not murder, did not commit adultery, and kept any vows they made, they were holy. And then Jesus started talking about anger, lust, and integrity! Why, Jesus' words challenged the very foundations of their ideas about holiness!

This, of course, is what bothered Karen. The people in her church emphasized behavior and seemed to feel that a person who followed the rules was holy. Deep down, Karen sensed that following rules can't make anyone holy; that holiness isn't a matter of rules at all. Somehow, holiness is an issue of the heart.

Karen was and is right about the rules her church emphasizes. But even more, Jesus' explanation means that implicit in the external boundaries established by God's Ten Commandments are internal boundaries which are far more significant for the people of God!

Transformation Required

When we shift our thinking about holiness from concern with external to internal boundaries, we seem even worse off than before! Aren't the internal boundaries much harder to maintain?

They would be.

Internal boundaries would be harder to maintain, if there was no forgiveness for stepping over the line. But in Christ you and I *have* forgiveness when we fail. The vision of God as Holy, Holy, Holy reminds us that when we see Him clearly we do sense our sinfulness. But we also recognize His forgiving and cleansing love. And we respond to that love with gratitude and a passion to please Him.

Internal boundaries would be harder to maintain if God did not intervene to work a change within us. But He has intervened! When we trust Jesus as Savior He does work a change within us. The Commandments which once were written on stone tablets are now being rewritten, etched on our living personalities.

Internal boundaries would be harder to maintain if we were forced to struggle with them on our own. But we are not! For God has given us His Holy Spirit, to guide and empower us for a life that is wholly pleasing to God.

Through the cleansing power of forgiveness, the inner renewal that accompanies salvation, and the dynamic aid of the Holy Spirit, we can be holy indeed.

FOR REFLECTION

1. How have you tended to think of holiness? In the Old Testament ritual and behavioral sense? Or in the New Testament internal and transformational sense?

_____

_____

_____

2. Do you suppose that Jesus' listeners were excited or dismayed when He "fulfilled" the Law in their hearing? Why?

_____

_____

_____

3. In the rest of this book we'll look at each of the Ten Commandments to discover the "fulfilled" meaning and describe the internal boundaries that help us live holy lives today. Do you have any personal goals you wish to set before you read on?

_____

_____

_____

Before going on to the next chapter, meditate on this comment on Jeremiah 31:31–34 from the Personal Growth™ Study Bible.

The contrast developed here is between Mosaic Law and a predicted "new covenant." Israel rightly celebrated the Law as a revelation of God's character and of His intent for human beings. Christians celebrate these aspects of the Law as well. But Israel saw obedience to the Law as a way to *become* righteous, despite centuries of failure to keep it.

Today Christians celebrate Christ's death as the initiation of the radically different New Covenant. Under the New Covenant God forgives our iniquities and writes His righteousness not on stone tablets but on human hearts.

Old and New Covenants represent two different ways of trying to relate to God. Israel misunderstood the Old and sought to establish a relationship with God based on human effort to be and to do good. The New Covenant clearly bases relationship with God on His readiness to forgive. The Old shows us righteousness. The New creates righteousness within us. As Christians we respect God's Law. But we rely on Christ to bring us peace with God.

NO OTHER GODS

*J*oanna has a god who answers every prayer—as long as Joanna meets seven "conditions." If her prayers aren't answered, it's because she failed to meet her god's conditions.

Leslie has a grandfatherly god, who mildly disapproves of some of her choices, but dotes on her so much that he'd never cause any real trouble.

Bob, whom we've already met, had a god who looked on disapprovingly no matter how hard Bob tried to please him.

If we were to ask, each one would say that the god he or she worships is God, the Creator, the Father of our Lord Jesus Christ. In a sense each would be right. But in another sense, each would be wrong. For another god has crowded in front of God. A god who wears a mask that distorts the face of the Lord.

Joanna's god is a compulsive deity. Rules are more important to him than relationships. He'll answer prayers if, and only if, his worshipper clears seven obstacles that he has erected. Joanna's god stands at the finish line, ready to reward winners with answers to prayer, and just as ready to disqualify anyone who trips over one of those obstacles and knocks over a hurdle in the dash to him for aid. Joanna's god, in making answers to prayer a matter of our successfully negotiating seven hurdles, has also limited himself. He's bound by his own rules to say "yes" to the request of a person who wins through his course. Answer to prayer is not a matter of bringing our requests to a wise Father and trusting in His love and judgment.

Leslie's god is a warm, friendly, and loving being. In fact, he is so loving that he isn't too upset when she sins. Of course, he has to disapprove. That's part of his job. But there's no way he'd get angry at her, or even let Leslie experience any consequences of her actions. Leslie's god is pretty ineffectual, actually. But he does appreciate it when Leslie finds time to drop in to church to say "Hi."

Bob's god is very different from Leslie's. His god is always demanding, usually angry, and totally disgusted with Bob. No matter how hard Bob tries to please his god, and Bob really does try, he just can't live up to his god's expectations. As a result, Bob always feels guilty and inadequate.

Old Testament Times

In Old Testament times challengers to God were relatively easy to recognize. They were the existing deities of pagan peoples. Archaeological research has identified many characteristics of these gods.

Pagan gods were not universal deities. They were associated with particular localities, which they were thought to own or control. Thus the Baal Peor (Deut. 4:3) was the locality controlled by the deity (Baal) associated with Peor; Baal Hazor (2 Sam. 12:23) the locality controlled by the deity (Baal) associated with Hazor, etc.

Pagan gods were not self-sufficient. The pagans had pantheons with multiple deities, to each of which certain characteristics or qualities were ascribed. Thus there might be a god of war, a goddess of childbirth, etc. No single god or goddess was thought of as complete in himself or herself.

Major pagan deities were associated with fertility. Baal, the male deity of the Canaanites, had as his consort Ashtoreth, a female deity. The pagans supposed that the fertility of the land depended on the enthusiastic sexual congress of their deities. There was a strong sexual component to their worship, with male and female prostitutes dedicated to the service of their deities, responsible by their sex acts for arousing the lust of the gods.

Pagan gods were thought of as having human vices as well as virtues. One pagan poem pictures Ashtoreth glorying in pools of blood trampled from her victims. When the prophets of Baal struggled on Mount Carmel to meet the challenge of Elijah (1 Kin. 18), the text tells us that they "cut themselves with knives and lances, until the blood gushed out on them" (v. 28). Why? Because the Baal they worshiped was thought to be a brutal god who loved the smell of human blood, and his prophets were desperate to attract their deity's attention.

In Old Testament times the mask that human beings held up before the face of the true God was grotesque indeed. To the pagans "god" was a local deity, so incomplete that it took multiple deities to reflect all the qualities of godhood. To the pagans "god" shared the vices and virtues of humanity, including an unbridled interest in immoral sex and an attraction to gratuitous violence.

No wonder the First Commandment says "You shall have no other gods before Me" (Ex. 20:3). It was unthinkable that any pagan notion of God be held by God's people to mask His true face and give God's people a distorted idea of His nature and His character.

Today the grotesque masks of humankind's pagan past have been set aside or hung on the walls of museums. No one, not even contemporary pagans, conceives of God in such gross terms.

Perhaps it would be easier for us to deal with this commandment if the masks that were held up before God's face today were as obviously false. Instead, even among Christians, there are other, subtle masks.

The God we worship has revealed Himself to us!

Joanna's compulsive god, who runs his worshipers through an obstacle course each time one comes to him in prayer, is not the God of the Bible.

Leslie's grandfatherly, ineffectual god, who so dotes on people that he no longer cares how they behave, is not the God of the Bible.

Bob's fault-finding god, who watches closely to seize every opportunity to accuse his worshipers of sin, is not the God of the Bible.

Joanna, Leslie, and Bob have all placed another god *before* God, masking and distorting His face, and keeping them from knowing Him as He truly is.

The God of the Bible

The prelude to the Ten Commandments gives us important guidance. The first words of God quoted in Exodus 20 say, "I am the LORD your God, who brought you out of the land of Egypt, out of the house of bondage" (20:2). The God we worship is a God who has acted in history past, and *who has revealed Himself to us!*

This is the significance of the words "I am the LORD your God, who brought you out of the land of Egypt." God is the One who defines Himself by His actions, and explains Himself in the Word He has spoken to us. Every other god is an invention of the human mind; a reflection cast by our deeply felt need to understand the universe and find meaning.

The external boundary that the First Commandment established was a boundary intended to keep Israel from worshiping pagan deities or adopting pagan notions about the nature of God. The internal boundary that the First Commandment implies is more subtle, and yet more significant. It is a boundary that you and I must take seriously as we seek to develop our own understanding of God. Simply put, *we reject every idea about God that is not rooted in His revelation of Himself in Scripture*. If we are to be holy, we must begin by coming to know God for who He really is.

If we look back we can see how maintaining this boundary would change the lives of Joanna, Leslie, and Bob.

Joanna's ideas about prayer simply don't square with the Bible's teaching about God. When Christ brought up the subject of prayer, He began by contrasting His teaching with the common practice of the Pharisees. "When you pray," Jesus said, "pray to your Father . . ." (Matt. 6:6).

Jesus then drew a contrast with pagan practice, which assumed that constant repetition had a better chance of getting a god's attention. "Therefore do not be like them. For your Father knows the things you have need of before you ask Him" (Matt. 6:8).

Jesus then taught the disciples a pattern prayer. "In this manner, therefore, pray: Our Father in heaven . . ." (Matt. 6:9).

If we are to be holy, we must begin by coming to know God for who He really is.

What is striking about these verses is Jesus' consistent emphasis on *relationship*. "Pray to your Father." "Your Father knows your needs." "Pray, 'Our Father . . .'"

Our understanding and practice of prayer must begin with the realization that God is a Father to those of us who believe in Jesus!

As our Father, God loves us as any good parent loves his or her own boys and girls. As our Father, God is deeply concerned about our every need. As our Father, God wants only and always what is best for us.

A little later in this chapter Jesus points out that God takes care of the birds of the air and the flowers of the fields. How much more precious to Him we are than they! How utterly then we can trust Him to meet our every need.

When we approach prayer in light of God's revealed character as our Father, we see how distorted the "hurdles" approach to prayer is. Is God the umpire of some spiritual Olympics, putting us over hurdles, rewarding us when we clear them and disqualifying us when we stumble? The God who reveals Himself in Scripture most certainly is *not!* Through Jesus, God is our Father, and understanding this warm and wonderful relationship, the writer of Hebrews says "Let us therefore come boldly to the throne of grace, that we may obtain mercy and find grace to help in time of need" (Heb. 4:16).

If Joanna sees God as her Father when she prayed, she would come boldly, thankfully, and in complete trust that God's answer to her prayers will be an expression of His love, whether that answer is yes or no.

Leslie's idea of a kindly, impotent grandfather god clearly distorts God's revelation of Himself in Scripture. In part, Leslie's problem parallels that of the ancient pagan, who simply could not conceive of a deity who could be complete in himself. To Leslie, the idea of a loving god seems to remove the possiblity that he could have "negative" qualities. Surely a loving god would never *punish* people for sin! Surely a loving god could never be *angry* with her! Surely a loving god would never be upset about unfairness—unless, of course, he got upset with someone who was unfair to *her*.

But the God of Scripture *is* complete in Himself. He is loving, but also committed to do right. He is patient, but angered by injustice. As moral arbiter and judge of the universe He created, God does not, and will not, overlook sins. In fact, God's hatred of sin is most clearly shown in history's ultimate loving act! God gave His only begotten Son to die as our substitute and pay for the sins we committed. If God were not loving, He would not have given His Son. If God were not moral judge of His universe, He would not have condemned His Son to death when Jesus took the full weight of our sins upon Himself.

Never assume that God hesitates to punish sin. But never forget that Jesus took our punishment, that we might have a Father/child relationship with God.

If Leslie saw God as the Scripture revealed Him, holy as well as loving, committed to righteousness as well as eager to forgive, her attitude toward her own sins would change. Leslie would begin to see her careless actions as God sees them, and would begin to stand in judgment of herself. Gradually Leslie's casual attitude toward sin would change, and she would begin to care about doing what is right and good.

Bob has recognized his mother as the source of his erroneous ideas about God. He has learned that God is no stern, disapproving parent, but a God of grace who takes delight in rewarding those who seek Him. It's been hard for Bob to see the Lord as a God of grace and realize that the stern, uncompromising looks his mother fixed on him as a child do not represent God at all.

But as Bob's understanding of God has grown and changed, the guilt and shame that drove him have been replaced by joyful gratitude. Bob continues to minister effectively to his congregation. But within, delight has replaced despair. Bob now senses God's love and grace infusing everything he does.

Living Within the First Commandment's Boundary

How do we today keep the First Commandment, "You shall have no other gods before Me"?

First, we realize that our ideas about what God is like can come from many sources. Our ideas about God can come from our parents and the way we were raised. Bob assumed that his mother's attitude toward him reflected God's attitude. And he was wrong!

Ideas about God can come from Christian friends and, yes, the pulpit. Joanna read a book about how to get her prayers answered. Because the author used Bible verses as proof texts, Joanna simply accepted what the author wrote without ever noticing that the book was distorting her concept of what God was like. Leslie got her idea about God from our secular culture, which likes the notion of a grandfatherly, irrelevant god. None of the three initially checked his or her image of God with Scripture to discover who God has revealed Himself to be.

The First Commandment invites us to begin our journey toward holiness by establishing a boundary through which no distorted ideas about God can pass. We establish this boundary by consciously searching God's Word to understand God on His own terms. We maintain this boundary by continually testing our ideas and practices for their essential agreement with God's revelation of Himself in His Word.

As we learn to live out this first of the Ten Commandments, we take a vital first step toward practical holiness.

FOR REFLECTION

1. Jot down three or four sentences that express ideas about God which have affected your life.

_____

_____

_____

2. Identify the sentence which expresses the idea about God which has had the most impact on you.

_____

_____

_____

3. Spend time with a concordance and a book like The Zondervan Dictionary of Christian Literacy, which explores key concepts of our faith. What does the Bible say about the idea of God which you

have identified above. Is your idea about God in harmony with
what God has revealed of Himself in Scripture? Or has that idea
functioned as another god "before" God which has masked His
true nature from you?

_____

_____

_____

*Before reading the next chapter in this book, meditate on this article
on John 8:42–47 from the* Personal Growth™ *Study Bible.*

In both Old and New Testament languages the word
for "truth" emphasizes the harmony of what is said with
reality. Something is true because it represents the way
things really are. When Jesus said "I tell the truth," He
claimed that what He taught was in complete harmony
with reality as God alone knows it to be.

Jesus' listeners assumed that they had the right to
stand in judgment on the truth of what Jesus said. Instead, Jesus' truth stands in judgment on them! Those
who heard and believed took their stand with Abraham,
who believed God. Those who heard and did not believe
took their stand with Satan, who from the beginning
rejected the truth in favor of lies, and thus were in Satan's
"family."

Today, too, the words Jesus spoke divide human
beings into two families: the family of God, and the family
of Satan. There is no neutral ground.

NO LIKENESS
OF ANYTHING

I'm not a devotee of radio or TV preachers. For one thing, I just don't have the time to listen to or watch them, or much else that comes on the television. But there is one colorful, charismatic southern evangelist I really enjoy listening to. In fact, I play his audio tapes while driving.

What I enjoy isn't just his vital delivery and creative images. I enjoy *him*. He's a good brother, whose loving spirit shows through, and whose wisdom often strikes a chord in my heart.

It's not that I always agree with him. In fact, quite often I don't agree. For instance, in one of his messages my good brother suggests that the reason we don't have perfect health and plenty of money in the bank is that we don't claim these blessings NOW. These things are our right, my brother believes. The only thing that keeps us from enjoying material blessings is the lack of faith we demonstrate by asking God to provide them *sometime*. What we are to do, he says, is to claim the promised blessings NOW. Do that, and we'll see God in the blessings He absolutely showers upon us.

The Need to See God

When Moses was on Mount Sinai being instructed by the Lord and given the Ten Commandments, all the people of Israel waited at the base of the mountain. When the Israelites had first camped at Sinai they were awe-struck. God shrouded the top of the mountain in dark, roiling clouds. Thunder rumbled and lightning bolts flashed constantly, their red glow reflecting against the clouds like some volcanic fire. The mountain itself shook. Heat radiated from it as from a furnace, as the clouds rose higher and higher. Then, framing this awesome sight, came a loud, penetrating sound, the sound of a trumpet blown endlessly, growing louder and louder as God Himself called out to Moses and spoke to him in a great voice.

At that moment the people fell back, fearful and trembling, only too eager to have Moses approach God alone. Moses could go to the top of that terrifying mountain to meet with God. The people would gladly wait on the plains below.

And so they did.

Moses trudged up the mountain until he was lost from sight, covered by the clouds that hid God from view. And the people on the plains settled down to wait.

But Moses delayed his return.

Days passed.

Finally, uncertain about what had happened to Moses, a delegation from the people came to Aaron, Moses' brother. "Come," the people said, "make us gods that shall go before us; for as for this Moses, the man who brought us up out of the land of Egypt, we do not know what has become of him" (Ex. 32:1).

Aaron, always weak when separated from the stronger Moses, agreed. The people brought golden earrings, and Aaron used their contributions to fashion a golden calf. When the calf was finished, the people were delighted.

"This is your god, O Israel!" they shouted to each other (v. 4).

"This is your god, . . . that brought you out of the land of Egypt" (v. 8).

So Aaron built an altar in front of the statue of the golden calf and announced a holiday. "Tomorrow," Aaron said. "Tomorrow we'll have a ceremony dedicated to the Lord. Be here early! We'll have sacrifices and offerings, and a great feast. We'll party!"

Looking back now we wonder how Aaron and the people of Israel could have done such a thing. How could they worship a gold calf and imagine that this thing they had made themselves had brought them out of Egypt? Today we know that they weren't quite that unsophisticated.

The sites in the ancient Middle East where deities were worshipped typically featured symbolic objects. A pole represented Ashteroth. A bull or calf formed of bronze or gold often represented Baal. It's not that the people thought the metal figure *was* the deity. It *represented* the deity. Quite often the invisible god was thought to attend his worship by standing on the back of the bull, an animal chosen to represent the deity because of its powerful build and strength.

Somehow though, the material representation seemed necessary. The people needed to *see* something. They needed some material representation of God.

Even Moses wasn't immune from the desire to see God. Exodus 33:18 describes Moses' request, "Please, show me Your glory." God responded by telling Moses, "I will make all My goodness pass before you, and I will proclaim the name of the LORD before you . . . ." But He said, "You cannot see My face" (33:19, 20).

We can experience God's goodness.

We can hear and know Him by name.

But we cannot, will not, as men and women living in this world, see God's face.

Seeing God in Old Testament Times

The Second Commandment is explicit, expressed in more detail than the first.

> You shall not make for yourself a carved image—any likeness of anything that is in heaven above, or that is in the earth beneath, or that is in the water under the earth; you shall not bow down to them nor serve them. For I, the LORD your God, am a jealous God.
>
> *Exodus 20:4, 5*

There is to be no material representation of the invisible God. God's people are not to bow down to any material object which purports to represent Him.

The boundary this command established for God's Old Testament people was clear and simple, unmistakable in its intent. Don't worship idols.

Human beings throughout history have demonstrated a perverse need to see God. They have devised a variety of ways to represent Him. Isaiah, in a powerful passage, ridicules the assumption that an idol can possibly represent God.

The blacksmith with the tongs works one in the coals.
Fashions it with hammers,
And works it with the strength of his arms.
Even so, he is hungry, and his strength fails;
He drinks no water and is faint.

The craftsman stretches out his rule,
He marks one out with chalk;
He fashions it with a plane,
He marks it out with the compass,
And makes it like the figure of a man,
According to the beauty of a man, that it may
    remain in the house.
He cuts down cedars for himself,
And takes the cypress and the oak;
He secures it for himself among the trees of the forest.
He plants a pine, and the rain nourishes it.

Then it shall be for a man to burn,
For he will take some of it and warm himself;
Yes, he kindles it and bakes bread;
Indeed, he makes a god and worships it;
He makes it a carved image, and falls down to it.
He burns half of it in the fire;
With this half he eats meat;
He roasts a roast, and is satisfied.
He even warms himself and says,
"Ah! I am warm, I have seen the fire."
And the rest of it he makes into a god,
His carved image,
He falls down before it and worships it.
Prays to it and says,
"Deliver me, for you are my god!"

They do not know nor understand.

Isaiah 44:12–18

Not only is the boundary established for God's Old Testament
people clear—worship no idol—the rationale behind it is clear. It
is simply impossible for any material object to represent God.
And it is utterly impossible for any material object to do for the
worshiper what God can do.

Seeing God in Our Day

Sarah, the cleaning lady, is excited. She's just gotten a letter from a TV minister to whom she's contributed before. Yes, this letter too asked for money. But this time the letter is special. The TV minister has claimed the promise that when we cast our bread on the water, God will return it a hundredfold. What's special is that the TV minister has *claimed this promise for her!* If Sarah will show her faith by sending the TV pastor $77 right away, God will return her, not $77, not $770, but a full $7,700! What's most exciting to Sarah is that her old car has been having a lot of trouble recently. She's been praying about getting a new car. Now, with the $7,700 her contribution of $77 guarantees, she'll be able to get a better vehicle than she imagined!

It is utterly impossible for any material object to do for the worshiper what God can do.

Today Sarah will be cleaning at the home of a Christian attorney. It's a new home and a beautiful one. She often chats with the attorney's wife as she works. What Sarah likes about her is that the woman doesn't act as if she's better than Sarah just because she's well off. Sarah doesn't even envy the woman her lovely home. After all, the attorney's wife has made it clear that she sees her home as an answer to prayer and as "evidence of God's favor."

"My husband works so hard," the attorney's wife commented one day. "He's always given time to serve the Lord and help people. He deserves the house that God has given us. I'm just thankful we can see how good God is as we look around each day."

Both Sarah and the friend she works for are sincere Christians. Each loves the Lord and does her best to serve Him. Neither one has any idea that she's inadvertently crossed a boundary established by the Second Commandment.

The external boundary the Second Commandment establishes is an obvious one. Don't worship idols. The internal boundary is far less obvious, but just as clear. *Nothing material is to represent God to me.* Now, certainly we're to see God's loving Hand in all the blessings we experience. And it's only right that we should thank and worship Him for His many good gifts.

Our problem with the Second Commandment comes when we begin to confuse the good things God gives with God. Our problem comes when we depend on God's good gifts as "the" proof of God's presence with us, so that when those good gifts are not to be found or are in short supply, we think God has abandoned us or no longer loves us.

Sarah has confidence that the $77 she plans to send in today will bring her $7,700. She doesn't know just how God will do it. But when that money comes, she will see God in it.

Sarah's friend is thankful for her new home. She loves it dearly. But most important is that to her the house represents God's favor. The house is proof positive that God loves them; that He cares.

I understand their feelings. I was in the Navy when I got my first car. I hesitated for months before I finally bought it. I wanted a car so badly that I was afraid it might begin to take the place in my life that I reserved for God. Would I begin to make choices based on my possession of the car? Would the car become too important to me?

I was still concerned when I bought it, a used 1951 Nash Rambler, for just $500. But driving from my parents' home in Michigan back to New York, where I was stationed, I made a wonderful discovery. I didn't *care* about the car!

Oh, I was glad to have it. But it didn't *matter* to me. Whether I had that car or lost it, I would still be the same. And God would be the same to me. *No material object could possibly represent God! Or displace Him in my heart.*

In 2 Corinthians 11 the apostle Paul recounts some of his experiences as a minister of Christ. "From the Jews five times I received forty stripes minus one. Three times I was beaten with rods; once I was stoned; three times I was shipwrecked; a night and a day I have been in the deep; in journeys often, in perils of waters, in perils of robbers, in perils of my own countrymen, in perils of the Gentiles, in perils in the city, in perils in the wilderness, in perils in the sea, in perils among false brethren; in weariness and toil, in sleeplessness often, in hunger and thirst, in fastings often, in cold and nakedness—

besides the other things, what comes upon me daily: my deep concern for all the churches" (11:24–28).

Yet this same Paul wrote to the Philippians from prison, "I have learned in whatever state I am, to be content" (4:11).

The Second Commandment had become an inner boundary for Paul that kept his heart content. No material thing could possibly represent God to him! At times even Paul felt intense pressure and was near despair (2 Cor. 1:8–9). Yet when he hurt the most, the apostle never supposed that God had abandoned him. The apostle Paul found contentment in a relationship with Jesus that did not depend on material blessings to be real.

God is a God who loves us completely and who loves us always. In *every* circumstance.

You and I too are to set the Second Commandment as a boundary within our hearts. We're to trust the God who loves us no less when tragedies befall us. We're to sense God's loving presence in poverty as well as wealth, in sickness as well as in health. God, the invisible One who has revealed Himself to us in Scripture, is a God who loves us completely and who loves us always. In *every* circumstance of our lives.

With the Second Commandment set as a boundary within our hearts, we will never doubt His love, or confuse His many blessings with Him.

FOR REFLECTION

1. How greatly have your circumstances tended to affect your feelings about God and His love?

_____

_____

_____

2. Why do you think people are so likely to see material blessings or good health as evidence of God's favor?

_____

_____

_____

3. How do you think setting the Second Commandment as a boundary within your own heart could contribute to your living a holy life?

_____

_____

_____

Before reading the next chapter, meditate on the following insight on Hebrews 12:7–15, taken from the Personal Growth™ Study Bible.

Parents usually look at Hebrews 12 for guidelines on how to discipline. But the passage is really intended to remind us how to deal with our own hard times. What principles apply?

Let's remember that "chastening" [hard times] is experienced by all God's children. In permitting them, God is motivated by love. His intent is that our hard times might promote holiness. God designs our hard times as training, which later produces "the peaceable fruit of righteousness."

But the benefit we receive from God's discipline depends on how we respond to it. Rather than become discouraged and give up, we are to meet hard times with courage. Rather than become bitter, we are to remember that hard times, like our blessings, are evidence of the grace of a God whose love for us is beyond compare.

TAKING GOD'S NAME IN VAIN

*F*rank was nervous.

He was about to take a stand. And it was kind of scary.

Frank worked at the post office as a mail carrier. Every morning as he sorted the day's mail, expertly slipping letters and bills into the compartments that represented the homes on his route, he and the other carriers chatted. They talked about politics and fishing. They complained about the cost of keeping their cars on the road. They argued about their favorite sports teams and made jokes about each other's looks. But what bothered Frank was that their conversation was constantly punctuated with four-letter words and frequent exclamations misusing God's name.

Frank had had just about all the "Je-zus" and "God!" that he could put up with.

But what was the best way to confront them? Frank had rehearsed over and over several different things he might say. But he still wasn't sure what was best. He went over his options again in his mind.

> "Hey, fellas. I'd appreciate it if you wouldn't use Jesus' name as a cussword."
>
> "Guys, you don't know Who you're talking about. Would you like me to introduce you?"
>
> "Did you know that you're breaking the Third Commandment?"
>
> "Don't you think it would be good to show a little more respect for God? You know, one day you're going to have to answer to Him."

Somehow none of the things Frank could think of to say seemed quite right. But he was going to say *something*. He just wasn't going to put up with them using God's name in vain any longer.

I suspect we've all felt a lot like Frank. We live in a society where God's name is treated with utter disrespect. No contemporary movie, even for the most general audience, seems complete without throwing in a "God!" or "Jesus!" here or there. "God!" has joined the "f-word" as a favorite way for sixth and seventh graders to indicate they think they're old enough to be part of adult society. The casual disregard for God's name that was characteristic of the locker room a few decades ago has spread to today's living rooms and every workplace. Despite the fact that almost eighty-eight percent of Americans claim to believe in God, it seems that ninety percent of the people we overhear quite unconsciously use His name as a swearword!

> The casual disregard for God's name has spread to today's living rooms and every workplace.

The Case of Hananiah

For years Jeremiah had been faithfully warning Judah. God had determined to destroy Jerusalem and its temple, and send the people off to Babylon as captives. Jeremiah's words had proven partly accurate, as the wealth of the temple and many of the upper class had already been deported to Babylon. But rather than being taken more seriously, Jeremiah was despised by his fellow countrymen and condemned as unpatriotic.

One afternoon, when Jeremiah publicly repeated his familiar warning, he was interrupted by Hananiah, the son of Azur. They were in the temple court at the time, surrounded by priests and people, when Hananiah began to shout.

> Thus speaks the LORD of hosts, the God of Israel, saying: "I have broken the yoke of the king of Babylon. Within two full years I will bring back to this place all the vessels of the LORD's house, that Nebuchadnezzar king of Babylon took away."

Jeremiah 28:2, 3

Hananiah continued to promise in God's name that the Lord would also return all the captives, including Judah's rightful king, Jeconiah.

Jeremiah, who was truly a patriot at heart, responded "Amen!" But as Jeremiah left the temple area, God spoke to him and sent him back to the court. So Jeremiah returned and confronted Hananiah.

> Thus says the LORD of hosts, the God of Israel: . . . "Hear now, Hananiah, the LORD has not sent you, but you make this people trust in a lie. Therefore thus says the LORD, 'Behold, I will cast you from the face of the earth. This year you shall die, because you have taught rebellion against the LORD.'"
>
> *Jeremiah 28:14–16*

Two months later Hananiah was dead!

The story is fascinating for the insight it provides into the Third Commandment. As they spoke, both Hananiah and Jeremiah used the same formula: "Thus says the LORD of hosts, the God of Israel." Each spoke in God's name. Each used a formula that claimed divine authority for his statement. The difference was that God had not spoken to Hananiah—and God had spoken to Jeremiah.

But why would Hananiah wrap the mantle of divine authority around his words? Why would he risk God's disapproval to please the priests and people who so eagerly welcomed words they wanted to hear?

Never think of "God" without a deep awareness of the reality that His name represents.

The answer is found in the Hebrew word translated "in vain" in the Third Commandment. That word, *sawe'*, is found fifty-three times in the Old Testament. In each case it designates something that is without substance or worth. It describes something which is *unreal*.

When the Third Commandment says "You shall not take the name of the LORD your God in vain," it is simply telling us not to treat "God" as unreal or irrelevant. We are never to mention or even think of "God" without a deep awareness of the reality that His name represents.

Hananiah was so driven by a desire to deliver a popular message to his contemporaries that he treated "God" as irrelevant. God hadn't spoken to him. But what did that matter? After all, what did God have to do with his opportunity to become the center of attention? What did God have to do with the chance to become the most popular man in Jerusalem?

And so Hananiah used the sacred formula, "thus says the LORD, the God of Israel," for his own purposes, acting as if God were unreal or at the least irrelevant. But God *is* real. God spoke out through Jeremiah. And in two months Hananiah died.

This Is My Name Forever

Years before this incident, and some forty years before God gave the Ten Commandments, the Lord called Moses to the mission of freeing Israel from slavery in Egypt. Moses, then eighty years old and for forty years a shepherd in the Sinai wilderness, tried to beg off. He offered excuse after excuse. He wasn't eloquent. The Israelites wouldn't believe God had sent him. Who was Moses anyway? A nobody. God, send someone else! Please!

It was then that God told Moses His name, Yahweh. The name is translated in Exodus 3:14 as I AM WHO I AM and simply as I AM. Everywhere else in our Old Testament where this special name appears, our English text simply says "the LORD," with the letters o-r-d rendered in small capital letters. As the passage continues, God tells Moses that this special name is "My name forever," "My memorial to all generations" (3:15). Other versions express this thought, "this is the Name by which I am to be remembered to all generations."

But what does "the LORD," or Yahweh, mean? The name is constructed of four Hebrew consonants and is a form of the verb "to be." Perhaps the best way to understand the name is to say that Yahweh means, "the One who is Always Present."

Exodus 6:3 contains an interesting comment. God says to Moses, "I appeared to Abraham, to Isaac, and to Jacob, as God Almighty, but *by* My name LORD I was not known to them." It's not that "Yahweh" does not appear in the Genesis documents. It's not even that Abraham may not have heard the Name. It is the *meaning* of the Name which they did not know by experience.

What was different about the Exodus generation to whom the Name is to be revealed? It was for this generation, powerless as slaves in the land of Egypt, that God would burst into history in an unmistakable way. Through a series of shattering plagues God would demonstrate once and for all that He cannot be relegated to some distant "spiritual" realm. God is by our side in this our world of space and time, vital, powerful, real. The Lord is the One who is Always Present With Us; not then, not now, and never an empty, meaningless word.

When the Third Commandment says "You shall not take the name of the LORD your God in vain," its use of the revelatory, relational name Yahweh, Lord, is significant. It was the name which God gave to Moses to communicate to His people. Then, now, and forever to believers "God" is filled with meaning. And that meaning is, our God is both real and present with us.

With Us

Frank is bothered by the casual and profane use of "Jesus" and "God" by his coworkers. It bothers him. And he's sure that they are breaking the Third Commandment. Frank doesn't realize that they're not breaking the Third Commandment at all.

Look at the language of the commandment more closely. It is addressed to Israel, God's own people. And it says, "*You* shall not take the name of the LORD *your God* in vain." The commandment isn't addressed to the habitually swearing non-Christians. This commandment is addressed to us, to believers! God isn't at all concerned that those who have no belief in or relationship with Him use words like "God" and

"Jesus" as if they are meaningless. After all, those names *are* meaningless to nonbelievers!

What God is deeply concerned about is that all too often those of us who do believe act as if the name of "the Lord *your* God" is empty and meaningless. Because God is One who is Always Present, God is always relevant in every situation!

Are you going to school? The Lord, as One who is Always Present, is relevant to your studies. You are to take your studies seriously and make every effort to excel.

Are you employed? The Lord, as One who is Always Present, is relevant to your job. You are to do your best for your employer, aware that your true employer is God and that it is your privilege to serve and please Him.

Are you married? The Lord, as One who is Always Present, is relevant to your marriage. As a husband or wife you are to commit yourself fully to your spouse, to love and support him or her and seek only his or her best.

Are you involved in some ministry? The Lord, as One who is Always Present, is relevant to your ministry. As His servant you are to seek always to glorify Him, never to win the accolades of other believers or for some other personal end. Hananiah, the prophet who spoke in the name of the Lord although the Lord had not sent him, tried to *use* God to gain his own ends. And fully merited the repayment he received.

Perhaps the one time Christians are most likely to use the name of the Lord in vain is when we pray. How often as we conclude our prayers we tack on the phrase, "in Jesus' name. Amen."

In Bible times, a name was more than a label. The name of a thing or a person was linked to its essence, to the character of the thing named. When Jesus encouraged the apostles to pray in His name (John 14:13, 14; 15:16; 16:23, 24, 26) He wasn't suggesting they use an add-on phrase. To pray in Jesus' name means to sense Him as Present with us, so that we identify the content and motivation of our prayers with all that Jesus is. To pray in Jesus' name means to pray with complete confidence that He who is Present With Us can and will act on our behalf in this world of space and time.

Israel understood the Third Commandment as an external boundary that was not to be crossed. Hananiah crossed it when he spoke in the name of the Lord although the Lord had not spoken to him. Hananiah's attempt to use the name of the Lord to gain a reputation and popularity showed how unreal and irrelevant he supposed God to be.

Today the Third Commandment is to be a boundary that you and I set up within our hearts to keep us close to God. It is a boundary that we never want to cross. It is a boundary that enables us to remember at all times, in every circumstance, that the Lord is present with us, and that the Lord is real.

Frank, as he puts up his letters in the post office, can set up this boundary in his heart. He'll still hear the cursing of his coworkers. But perhaps, rather than being upset, Frank will remember that the Christ who is Present with him is far more concerned with the spiritual condition of Frank's friends than with their language. And perhaps Frank will begin to pray for them in Jesus' name, identifying himself with Christ's passion to love and win the lost.

FOR REFLECTION

1. How many ways can you think of that Christians can take the name of the Lord, as explained in this chapter, "in vain"?

_____

_____

_____

2. When are you most likely to feel that God is irrelevant to a situation in which you find yourself?

_____

_____

_____

3. What difference would it make in your life if you were constantly aware that God is not only Present with you but that He is relevant and able to act in any situation?

_____

_____

_____

Before going on to the next chapter, meditate on the following insight into Psalm 94 from the Personal Growth™ *Study Bible.*

Anxiety has been defined as a feeling of apprehension, worry, or tension. Some of us feel anxious and threatened even though nothing seems seriously wrong. This has been called neurotic, in contrast to normal, anxiety. If our employer is laying people off, or we're due to go to the doctor to get results of a series of tests, it's normal to feel anxious. This anxiety goes away when the situation is resolved.

But the psalmist seems to suggest that for some of us, neurotic anxiety is normal! He confesses to a "multitude of my anxieties within me." Like the psalmist, those of us troubled with anxiety need not feel guilt. Anxiety is not an indication of spiritual failure. The psalmist even finds his anxious moments a time of triumph. Despite them, God's "comforts delight my soul." Anxieties may give us unusual opportunities to learn trust. As the rest of the psalm reminds us, God is trustworthy. He sees. God knows. God is with us. In God we find rest.

REMEMBER THE SABBATH

Jim fidgeted in his seat.

Betty Jo gave him one of her looks.

Jim looked away, glanced at his watch, and then looked up at the preacher again. Why was the pastor so long-winded, anyway?

This was the season when Jim felt frustrated almost every Sunday morning. And the season when Betty Jo wished she'd married someone else. Anyone else but a football freak like Jim.

"Darn," Jim thought. "I'll miss the kickoff for sure. And it's the Bears and Green Bay!"

Jim twisted again in the pew, bumping into Betty Jo and getting a sharp elbow in the ribs in return. This time Betty Jo didn't look over at her husband. She just stared grimly at the pastor. He *was* long-winded, almost every Sunday. But Betty Jo knew very well if the first game on the TV today had been Pittsburgh and Cleveland, the sermon would have been really short.

"Men," Betty Jo thought. "They're all alike."

When Christians debate the appropriate way to spend Sunday, someone is sure to go back to Exodus and quote the Fourth Commandment. "Remember the Sabbath day, to keep it holy" (Ex. 20:8). Someone else will quickly point out that this is the only one of the Ten Commandments that isn't repeated in some form in the New Testament. If the debate goes on long enough, a variety of Bible verses will fly back and forth.

"Yes, but Jesus said the Sabbath was made for man and not man for the Sabbath in Mark 2:27. It's a day of rest, and watching football is restful!"

"Come on! Jesus wasn't talking about football! In Matthew 12:10–12 He was telling the Pharisees it was all right for Him to heal on the Sabbath. That it's OK to do good."

"That's all well and good. But you sound just like the Pharisees who made up all those rules about what you could and couldn't do on the Sabbath. This is the age of grace, not law!"

"Now that's a weak excuse. God instituted the Sabbath at Creation. That's a really long time before the Law was introduced. It's the principle of setting a day aside for God that's important. And you gotta face it. God isn't playing quarterback for the Chicago Bears!"

"Oh, yeah? Well how about Romans 14. It says in verses 5 and 6 that it's OK for someone to think of one day as being special and OK for someone else to see all days as alike. I just think *every* day is the Lord's day, not just one day a week!"

While the "how do we keep Sunday" debate often degenerates into a competition to see who can come out looking the most spiritual, the issues involved are real. Why did God, in the Ten Commandments, tell Israel to set one day of the week aside? And what does keeping the Sabbath—or Sunday!—have to do with holiness?

External Boundaries?

The Fourth Commandment required Israel to keep the Sabbath as a holy day. The one defining characteristic of keeping the Sabbath that we find in the text has to do with work.

> Six days you shall labor and do all your work, but the seventh day is the Sabbath of the LORD your God. In it you shall do no work: you, nor your son, nor your daughter, nor your male servant, nor your female servant, nor your cattle, nor your stranger who is within your gates. For in six days the LORD made the heavens and the earth, the sea, and all that is in them, and rested the seventh day. Therefore the LORD blessed the Sabbath day and hallowed it.
>
> *Exodus 20:9–11*

The external boundary established in this commandment seems a simple one. "You shall do no work." But this simple phrase led to endless discussion in first-century Judaism and is still debated today. Just what constitutes "work"? What is lawful for God's people to do on the Sabbath, and what is not lawful?

The *Mishna* is an important, six-part codification of rules intended to guide the Jewish people as they seek to keep God's Law. It records the sayings of rabbis of the first and second centuries A.D., and reflects the approach to the Law taken by the Pharisees of Jesus' day. It contains many intense discussions of Sabbath-keeping. Included is this list defining "work" prohibited on the Sabbath: (1) he who sows, (2) plows, (3) reaps, (4) binds sheaves, (5) threshes, (6) winnows, (7) selects (fit from unfit produce or crops), (8) grinds, (9) sifts, (10) kneads, (11) bakes, (12) he who shears wool, (13) washes it, (14) beats it, (15) dyes it, (16) spins, (17) weaves, (18) makes two loops, (19) weaves two threads, (20) separates two threads, (21) ties, (22) unties, (23) sews two stitches, (24) tears in order to sew two stitches, (25) he who traps a deer, (26) slaughters it, (27) flays it, (28) salts it, (29) cures its hide, (30) scrapes it, and (31) cuts it up, (32) he who writes two letters, (33) erases two letters in order to write two letters, (34) he who builds, (35) he who tears down, (36) he who puts out a fire, (37) he who kindles a fire, (38) he who hits with a hammer, (39) he who transports an object from one domain to another.

While the list looks exhaustive, it is only the beginning! Take plowing. What constitutes plowing? What if you spit on soft ground and move the soil? The rabbis decided this was plowing, and if you did it, you broke the Sabbath prohibition against work. But if you spit on a rock, and no soil was moved, you were all right.

An ancient debate translated into modern terms relates to dyeing cloth. One rabbinic school held that if you put cloth in a vat of dye before the Sabbath began, and took it out afterward, no work was involved. But a competing rabbinic tradition argued that since the process of dyeing was going on during the Sabbath, even if you put the cloth in before the holy day and took it out afterward, you violated the Law's prohibition against work. In modern terms, one rabbinic school holds that while you cannot turn on an electric appliance on the Sabbath, you can put it on a timer which will turn it on automatically! The other rabbinic tradition holds that causing the electricity to flow on the Sabbath, whether you set the timer before or not, violates the prohibition against work.

This background of Jewish thinking about the Fourth Commandment helps us understand why the Pharisees were so upset when Jesus' disciples, walking on a path beside a wheat field, reached out and plucked some heads of grain to eat. While this action is specifically permitted in the Law (Deut. 23:25), the Pharisees immediately charged Jesus' followers with law-breaking (Matt. 12). According to the complex rulings generations of rabbis had devised, the disciples were *reaping!* And that was *work!* To the Pharisees this was tantamount to breaking God's Law, and they were honestly shocked that Jesus would permit it.

The boundaries which promote holiness are internal, not external, and have been so from the beginning!

Jesus rejected their interpretation and their approach to Scripture itself, which focused on defining external boundaries which a person must not cross. A person might live his entire life within this kind of boundary and still not be holy! In quoting Hosea 6:6, "I desire mercy and not sacrifice," Jesus shifted the focus from external observance of rules to internal attitudes of the heart. The boundaries which promote holiness are internal, not external, and have been so from the beginning!

And, if anyone challenged Jesus' authority to make this kind of statement, Christ said simply, "the Son of Man is Lord even of the Sabbath" (Matt. 12:8). Jesus, as Lord, instituted the Sabbath! Who had a greater right to point out where Israel had gone wrong?

Internal Boundaries

The first three of the Ten Commandments (see Ex. 20:3–8) also explore relationship with God. If we are to be truly holy, we must begin here, nurturing and developing intimacy with Him. As we've explored the commandments we've seen that while each of the ten established an external boundary for Israel, each also implies a far more significant internal boundary for believers of every era.

The First Commandment, "You shall have no other gods before Me," calls us to purify our concept of God by subjecting every impression we have of Him to His self-revelation in the Scriptures.

The Second Commandment, "You shall not make for yourself a carved image," calls us to divorce our confidence in God's love from every material object we might be tempted to assume represents either His favor or His disfavor.

The Third Commandment, "You shall not take the name of the LORD your God in vain," calls us to be consciously and constantly aware that God is real, that He is with us, and that He can and will act for us. "God" is not an empty or meaningless word!

What then is the inner boundary that the Fourth Commandment calls us to establish? "Remember the Sabbath day," the commandment says, "to keep it holy." And the text goes on to explain, "Six days you shall labor and do all your work."

The answer is suggested in one of Jesus' most familiar parables. He described a sower going out to sow seed. As the man broadcast the seeds, scattering them with rhythmic sweeps of his arm, the seeds fell here and there. Some of the seeds Jesus described fell among thorns, which sprang up and choked them. Later Jesus explained, and contrasted these seeds with seeds which fell on "good ground."

> Now, he who received seed among the thorns is he who hears the word, and the cares of this world and the deceitfulness of riches choke the word, and he becomes unfruitful. But he who received seed on the good ground is he who hears the word and understands it, who indeed bears fruit and produces: some a hundredfold, some sixty, some thirty.
>
> *Matthew 13:22, 23*

Israel worshiped God on the Sabbath. During the Babylonian captivity, with the temple destroyed, there was a fresh and new emphasis on the study of Scripture. The synagogue system developed, and with it the conviction that the proper way to spend the Sabbath was in worship and study of the Word of God. The tragic flaw that developed was an increasing emphasis on Law-keeping, and on defining the external boundaries within which one might consider himself "holy."

After the resurrection of Jesus, the church abandoned the Sabbath [Saturday] to commemorate the resurrection of Christ on the Lord's Day, the first day of the Week [Sunday] (Luke 24:1; Acts 20:7). But taking time to set aside "work" and the "cares of this world" wasn't just a Sunday kind of thing. The Book of Acts has a description of the earliest Christians' lifestyle:

> So continuing daily with one accord in the temple, and breaking bread from house to house, they ate their food with gladness and simplicity of heart, praising God and having favor with all the people.
>
> *Acts 2:46, 47*

There was time to focus their thoughts, with others, on the Lord. There was time to meet and share over meals. There was time to praise God.

Throughout the Old Testament the Sabbath is closely associated with the greatest of God's acts. The Fourth Commandment is explicitly linked with Creation. God's people were given the Sabbath, "for in six days the Lord made the heavens and the earth, the sea, and all that is in them, and rested the seventh day." The Sabbath was a day that reminded Israel of Creation, and that the Lord their God was and is the source of all that exists.

The Fourth Commandment is explicitly linked with redemption from Egypt. "And remember that you were a slave in the land of Egypt, and the LORD your God brought you out from there by a mighty hand and by an outstretched arm; therefore the LORD your God commanded you to keep the Sabbath day" (Deut. 5:15).

The Fourth Commandment is explicitly linked to Israel's covenant relationship with God. "Speak also to the children of

The Fourth Commandment is linked to the greatest of God's acts: Creation, Exodus, Covenant.

Israel, saying: 'Surely My Sabbaths you shall keep, for it is a sign between Me and you throughout your generations, that you may know I am the LORD who sanctifies you'" (Ex. 31:13). The Sabbath was a day on which the Israelites were to remember that God had chosen them and set them apart to be His people.

The inner boundary that the Sabbath day set was a boundary that we need to establish for ourselves if we are to become a truly holy people. *We are to take time away from "work" and the cares of this life to focus our attention on God.* As the three passages above clearly teach, we are to contemplate the wonder of who God is and all He has done for us. Our God is the source of all that is. He is the One who has redeemed us. He is the One who has loved us and set us aside to be His own.

Whatever day we keep, if we are to be holy we must take time to contemplate and worship Him.

FOR REFLECTION

1. How do you use or misuse the opportunities that not having to work on Saturdays and Sundays provides?

_____

_____

_____

2. Do you think it would be wise for a church to establish rules for what the congregation should or should not do on Sunday? Why?

_____

_____

_____

3. How can you order your time to live within the inner boundary taught in the Fourth Commandment? Can you decide now to set aside specific times when you set aside "work" to simply meditate on and praise the Lord?

_____

_____

_____

Before going on to the next chapter, meditate on this insight into Matthew 11:28, 29, from the Personal Growth™ Study Bible.

There are times when everything presses in on us and we're simply overwhelmed. There's so much to do we'll never get it done. There's so much pain we'll never feel healed. We are so tired there's no way we can finish all we must do. At times like these Jesus comes to us with a familiar invitation. "Take my yoke upon you, all you who are weary and burdened, and I will give you rest."

The yoke of Bible times fit over the shoulders of animals who pulled a plow and distributed the weight. Jesus invites us to come alongside, to slip His yoke on our shoulders, and find rest. The promise is that when we choose to walk with Jesus, He walks with us. And He lends us the full weight of His strength.

The rest we find is not leisure. It is the peace which comes from knowing that, with Christ's help, we simply cannot be overcome.

HONOR PARENTS

*R*ichard doesn't like his mother.
In fact, he can't stand her.

His mother complains constantly. She shows no affection or appreciation for him now that she's in her late seventies. In fact, she never did! Even though Richard visits her faithfully, shops for her, and takes her to the doctor, Mom never mutters even one word of thanks.

Richard lived with his mother and stepfather during his childhood. They ran a neighborhood bar, and after school Richard was expected to show up and work. He wasn't paid, except with a cuff to the ear if he wasn't quick enough to respond to one of his stepdad's shouted demands. Supper was whatever sandwich Richard could make when he had a moment.

Looking back now, some forty years later, Richard honestly can't remember hearing a kind or loving word from either one.

Fran and Sis grew up in the same home, although Fran was six years older. Mom and Dad went to church regularly, and even sang in the choir. But both were alcoholics. Although Sis was never molested by her father, she can remember how frightening it was as a teenager to take a shower. Her dad had adjusted the lock on the bathroom door so he could open it and peek in at her whenever he wanted.

What was worse, of course, was that when Mom and Dad got drunk they fought. Dad, who had a physically taxing job in construction, would often beat Mom when that happened. Sis can remember cleaning up blood streaks from the floor after her dad dragged her mom through the house. Sis can also remember her mother shouting at her dad and cursing him after he'd visited a prostitute and given Mom syphilis.

By the time Sis was in junior high school she was rushing home after school to prepare supper. She knew that if her mom and dad ate supper early they'd be less likely to get drunk. If she didn't make supper and feed it to them, they'd sit at the table drinking with no food in their stomachs. Then they'd get drunk for sure, and Sis would have to run to her room, cover her ears, and try to keep out the sound of the shouts and blows that were sure to follow.

Holiness and the Commandments

The first four commandments, often called the First Tablet of the Law, speak about how we maintain a holy and healthy relationship with God. The last six commandments, the Second Tablet of the Law, are about how we maintain holy and healthy relationships with others. Both sets of commandments are *relational* and *interpersonal*.

Both sets of commandments establish boundaries. As we've seen, the boundaries set up for God's Old Testament people have a clear external definition. Don't adopt pagan notions about God. Don't worship idols. Don't misuse God's name. Don't work on the Sabbath.

But as Jesus made plain in His Sermon on the Mount, the external boundaries do not and cannot express God's full intent. To adequately understand the commandments we must look beyond the external boundaries that the Law established. To adequately understand holiness, we must explore what God looks for not in our behavior, but in our hearts. We must, then, search out the *internal* boundaries implied in each commandment.

The last six commandments are about how we maintain holy and healthy relationships with others.

We must establish these internal boundaries for ourselves and, enabled by the Holy Spirit's transforming power, learn to live within them. As a people set apart and dedicated to God, we are to *be holy* and not simply *behave* in outwardly holy ways.

Of course, it's hard enough to live within the external boundaries. That's something that first-century Israel knew only too well. The rabbis worked zealously to develop and define rules that would serve as a fence around God's Law. This passion lay behind many apparent extremes. Why worry about whether one spits on soft or hard ground? It was because the pious Jew was deeply, honestly concerned with keeping God's commandments. So, for instance, the "work" mentioned in the Fourth Commandment had to be thoroughly defined, even to the point of the ridiculous. Only in this way did the rabbis believe they could make absolutely, positively sure that the Law wasn't broken inadvertently.

However, the rabbis were practical men. In working out their definitions they dealt with many issues that, if too strictly interpreted, seemed to place unnecessary hardship on people. And many rabbis were truly humanitarian men.

Take, for instance, the matter of vows. Numbers 30:2 states, "if a man makes a vow to the LORD, or swears an oath to bind himself by some agreement, he shall not break his word; he shall do according to all that proceeds out of his mouth." If we take this ruling in its literal sense, and suppose that first-century Jews did likewise, we're left with the impression that the more than forty Jewish men mentioned in Acts 23 must have starved to death! The men bound themselves "under a great oath that we will eat nothing until we have killed [the Apostle] Paul" (Acts 23:12). Why, they even went to the chief priests and elders and told them about the "great oath" they had taken (23:14)!

Despite appearances, however, there is no chance at all that even one of them died from starvation or lack of water.

The Reference Guide to the Steinsaltz edition of the *Talmud* describes a rabbinic interpretive principle called *se'elat lehakam*, "a request [made] to a scholar." The reference guide explains, "If a person makes a vow or takes an oath, or consecrates property and afterwards regrets having done so, he may go to a scholar and request of him that he release him from the vow."[1]

Fascinating! And the Jerusalem *Talmud* even illustrates the principle with a story that closely parallels the Acts passage! It takes a person who vows not to eat. Now, if he eats, he sins against the vow. But if he doesn't eat, he sins against his life. So how do you avoid sinning in this situation? Why, you go before a sage, a biblical scholar, and he absolves you from the vow!

So the forty were never in danger of starving, however "great" their oath. There was always a way out. And they knew it!

It was something like this with the command to honor parents. The Jewish rabbis were convinced that the command to "honor" parents implied taking financial responsibility for them in their old age. In fact, a comment on this commandment in the *Talmud* says "A son is bound to feed his father, to give him drink, to clothe him, to protect him, to lead him in, and to conduct him out, and to wash his face, his hands, and his feet."

But the rabbis also had developed rules for making contributions to the temple. One tradition was that of *corban*, by which an individual dedicated possessions or money to the temple. The action was something like our placing of assets in trust. During his lifetime the person making the dedication retained the assets and derived the income from them. After his death the assets were transferred to the temple treasury.

And so someone, perhaps someone who had a parent like Richard or Fran and Sis, raised a question. The Fifth Commandment says I'm to support my father. But I've dedicated many of my possessions to the temple. Would it be right for me to take assets dedicated to God and use them to support my father? The sages considered the question and made their decision. It is reported, with Jesus' comment, in Mark 7:10–13:

> Moses said, "Honor your father and your mother";
> and "He who curses father or mother, let him be put
> to death." But you say, "If a man says to his father or
> mother, 'Whatever profit you might have received from me
> is Corban'—" (that is, a gift to God), then you no longer
> let him do anything for his father or his mother, making
> the word of God of no effect through your tradition which
> you have handed down. And many such things you do.

The great tragedy of rabbinic Judaism was and is that in seeking to define every external detail of life, not only has the inner meaning of the Law been lost, but the Word of God has frequently been set aside in favor of some rabbinic ruling!

Truly Honoring Our Parents

The Expository Dictionary of Bible Words in its study of the word "honor" agrees that financial support is one way in which parents are to be honored (see Prov. 3:9; 1 Tim. 5:8 as well as Mark 7). But the command to "honor" parents also implies listening to, respecting, and obeying them. While each of these has behavioral expressions, it's clear that "respecting" is essentially an *internal issue*. Honoring parents is a matter of fundamental attitude toward our mothers and fathers.

> The command to "honor" parents also implies listening to, respecting, and obeying them.

Richard honors his mother by visiting her, shopping for her, getting her medicine, and taking her to the doctor. But he can't help feeling bitter inside as he remembers the way she mistreated him as a child, and the way her sharp tongue still dissects him today. His stomach churns every time she calls, and he becomes more and more tense and irritable as a visit draws near.

Fran, who escaped the family household a half-dozen years before Sis, went up the hill to her parents' house once a week to shop for her mom and dad. They're old now, in or near their eighties. And Fran tries to be a good daughter. But often Fran finds herself lying awake at night, thinking back on her childhood, rehearsing things she wishes she'd said back then. Fran now drinks too much herself, and when she does she can feel the bile rising as bitter, hostile remarks—remarks Fran is sure that her mom especially deserved—come to mind.

What about Sis, who bore the brunt of her mother and dad's developing alcoholism all through her junior high and high school years? Sis calls her mom at least every other week. She sends flowers on birthdays, holidays, and anniversaries. Sis is well aware of her parents' flaws. But somehow she has a different perspective than Fran.

Today Sis realizes that her mother did the best she could. Mom had a lot of faults. She wasn't a caring person. But Mom did instill in her daughter traits that Sis appreciates. She expected Sis to do well in school. And Sis did. She expected

Sis to work hard. And Sis does. She expected Sis to be responsible and truthful. And Sis is.

Dad had faults too. He drank. He beat Mom. He was unfaithful. But Sis looks back and remembers that when she was small, Dad always seemed to have time for her. He'd sit on the porch and tell her stories. When the boys left home, he even made her his fishing buddy.

Sis had long ago confronted her parents and come to realize that they simply did not understand how they had hurt her. They were too caught up in their own twisted lives to be the parents she yearned for. When that realization came, Sis was able to step back, to understand, and even to have compassion.

Sometimes Sis wonders what it would have been like to grow up in that "ideal" Christian home we like to read and talk about. But Sis knows that many of her most important qualities grew out of the pain and frustration of her childhood and teen years. And she is truly thankful, to God, and to Mom and Dad.

There's a fascinating comment attached to the Fifth Commandment. "Honor your father and your mother, *that your days may be long upon the land which the* LORD *your God is giving you.*" Honoring our parents benefits *us!* God has given us this command not so much for the benefit of our mothers and fathers as for ourselves.

Looking at Richard and Fran and Sis, real people, although these are not their real names, we can see why. Sis has found the grace to see her parents as weak and fallible human beings, sinners who, as sinners do, have hurt both themselves and those they love. We are all sinners, but some are more tragic sinners than others. How tragic that Richard's mom is still the bitter, negative person that he remembers as a child. How tragic that Fran and Sis's mom and dad never knew the joy of a truly loving union or the peace that comes with mutual respect. When we look at our parents in this way, we not only find it in our hearts to understand, but to have compassion as well.

God has established a new boundary in Sis's heart as she relates to her parents. She will no longer cross over that boundary to feel bitter toward them. As she lives within the framework of what is truly meant by honoring parents, Sis continually finds her heart softened toward her mom and dad. And today she reaches out to them with a compassion and love that have brought healing—to her!

Richard and Fran, while honoring their parents outwardly, constantly cross the inner boundary established by the Fifth Commandment. They dwell on past hurts and are vulnerable to new ones. They do not and cannot seem to love their parents, or feel compassion for them. Somehow they have never opened up their hearts to God, or asked His Holy Spirit to free them from their bondage to the past by enabling them to forgive, and to love.

FOR REFLECTION

1. How does honoring parents, as explained in this chapter, promote our personal holiness?

_____

_____

_____

2. Why *must* the command to honor parents refer to inner attitude, and not simply to behaviors such as obeying or providing financial support?

_____

_____

_____

3. How were your parents like, or unlike, the parents described in this chapter? How would you describe your relationship with your parents?

_____

_____

_____

4. How will honoring parents affect one's relationship with them? As children? As teenagers? As adults?

_____

_____

_____

Before going on to the next chapter spend some time meditating on this commentary on 2 Samuel 18:33, taken from the Personal Growth™ Study Bible.

As David wept over his son Absalom he must have looked back, and wished he had done so many things differently. There was no comfort for David in the fact that ultimately it was Absalom's own choices which caused his death. We suffer with our children, and love them, however they may be to blame.

How do we handle family heartaches? Chapter 19 tells us that Joab rebuked the king and insisted he go out to comfort the living. David could grieve alone at night, and undoubtedly did. But there were others who needed him during the daylight hours. Because David was king, he had to think of them and their needs.

Grief and regret will touch all of us at some time. But like David, we must arise, and tend to the needs of the living. Only in this way will there be healing, for them—and for us.

---

1. *Talmud,* The Reference Guide to the Steinsaltz edition (New York, NY: Random House, 1989), 259.

9

YOU SHALL NOT MURDER

*T*he usual protesters stood by, gathered in twos and threes. When the TV truck rolled up outside the prison, they all grouped together. They lit their candles and held up their posters protesting the execution scheduled for one minute after midnight. One of the signs read, "Legalized murder!" and another proclaimed "No blood on our hands, please!"

The next morning a popular talk-show host took his first fifteen minutes to light into the protestors.

"This guy, this *scum*, raped and killed two old ladies! The problem isn't that after eleven years—yeah, eleven years—this guy got what he deserved. The problem is he wasn't convicted, sentenced, and executed *the next day!* The problem is that these bleeding-heart idiots can't see what's happening in this country. Hey, it isn't safe to walk the streets at night, and they want us to cry over some *killer?* How about the victims? Yeah, how about the innocent people who are scared to go out of their houses at night, afraid some punk with a gun will break into their houses? My God, you don't even dare honk your horn at some idiot who cuts you off on the highway for fear he'll pull up beside you and blow you away!

"It's not the death sentence that's a problem. It's the fact we send the wrong message to criminals. Commit a crime? Sure, we'll send you on a paid vacation where you can watch cable TV and play basketball all day. Or lift weights, so you can beat up on somebody when you get out. Kill somebody? Hey, it's all right. We'll let you out in five or ten or fifteen years. Even if you get sentenced to death, you'll sit around at our expense for years before you're executed—if you ever are. Come on, folks. Let's get with it before our society really goes to hell in a handbasket. We're halfway there now, and those idiots with their signs and candles and tears for some cold-blooded killer aren't helping one bit!"

Killing, or Murder?

Much of the debate over capital punishment hinges on an earlier mis-translation of the Sixth Commandment. The original King James read "thou shalt not kill." The New King James rightly translates, "You shall not murder." The difference is important.

The word *harag*, to be translated "kill," is typically used of the violent killing of any person by another. Cain killed Abel. Jezebel killed God's prophets. The people at Elijah's urging killed 450 prophets of Baal. God killed the firstborn of Egypt. Just this brief survey tells us that this word is used of justified and unjustified killing, and even of divine judgment. *Harag* simply describes killing as a fact, without making any specific judgment, though the context in which the word appears typically makes this clear.

> The Sixth Commandment prohibits murder, not every act of killing.

For instance, Genesis 9:5, 6 introduces the principle of social responsibility and says that one who kills a man is to be executed. Much later David ordered the killing [*harag*] of two men who had assassinated Saul's son and David's rival for the rule of Israel (2 Sam. 4:11, 12). According to Genesis 9 and other passages, David was not only right to order their execution, but as ruler he was morally responsible to execute them!

There is, however, another Hebrew word for killing, which has no parallel in other Middle Eastern languages. This word is *rasah*, and this is the word found in our commandment and in other Old Testament passages where murder and manslaughter are discussed (cf. Num. 35). When this word is used it identifies a particular killing as a *personal killing*. Of particular importance is the fact that this word is not used of killing in war, or of judicial execution. Personal killings, murder or manslaughter, fall in a different category entirely.

Numbers 35, where eighteen of the forty-seven Old Testament uses of *rasah* are found, carefully describes how Israel was to deal with personal killings. If a personal killing was accidental, done without hostility, the killer was to flee to a City of Refuge and live there safely for a specified time until he

or she could return home. If, however, a personal killing
was intentional, done with hostility, and hostility could be
established by the testimony of at least two witnesses, the
murderer was to be put to death. Numbers 35:31 sums up the
position of the Old Testament on personal killings. "Moreover
you shall take no ransom for the life of a murderer who is
guilty of death, but he shall surely be put to death."

The careful use of language in the Old Testament which
distinguishes between judicial and personal killings helps us
to think biblically about capital punishment and the specific
boundary established by the Sixth Commandment. But when
we read Old Testament case law, we find that there are positive
aspects to this commandment as well!

The Commandments and Case Law

Exodus 20 contains God's Ten Commandments, which
define holiness in broad terms, as principles that are to govern
our relationship with God and our relationships with other
persons. Immediately following, in chapters 21—23, are rulings
on many different "minor" matters. What if a person is gored
by a neighbor's ox? What if a fire breaks out and burns a
neighbor's field? What if someone is hurt in a fight? What if
you see the donkey of a person who hates you lying under its
burden?

At first it seems strange. Why go from the most profound
and basic principles of holiness to such, if you will, little things?

The answer is that the case law is included in the Old
Testament to *illustrate application of the principles*. It's fine to have
high moral standards. But unless we understand how to apply
those standards to the most mundane experiences of human
life, the principles we affirm will have no practical impact.
So the Lord through Moses gave Israel a lengthy series of
illustrations, both here and in other passages in Exodus and
Deuteronomy. In effect, God said, "Now, here is what these
commandments *mean*."

If we search through the case law in these chapters to
illustrate the Sixth Commandment, "You shall not murder,"
we do find a closer definition of the negative boundary. We are
not to raise our hand in hostility against another and cause his

death. But we are also not to testify falsely against another person so as to do him harm (23:2, 7).

But case law also has expressions of *positive boundaries* implied in the "you shall not murder" command. A person who digs a pit must cover it, lest even an animal fall in and be hurt (see Ex. 21:33, 34). Deuteronomy 22:8 says, "When you build a new house, then you shall make a parapet for your roof, that you may not bring guilt of bloodshed on your household if anyone falls from it." *The commandment not to murder implies actively seeking to protect the life and welfare of others!*

Jesus on Murder

Earlier we saw that Jesus kept His promise to fulfill the Law (to provide a full and complete and true explanation). He did this in a series of sayings, "You have heard it was said to those of old," and then going on, "But I say to you . . . ." In this series Jesus gave a number of illustrations, each of which shifts our attention from an external boundary established in Old Testament Law to an internal boundary that Jesus explains.

The truly holy person is one who is not hostile!

One of the themes of the older Law which Jesus dealt with is expressed in the Sixth Commandment: "You shall not murder." In quoting this commandment Jesus used the Greek word, *phoneuo*, which makes the same distinction between killing and murder that is made by the Old Testament term, *rasah*. According to Jesus, the Old Testament sets a boundary and warns that whoever crosses it "will be in danger of the judgment" (Matt. 5:21). But the real issue addressed by the Sixth Commandment is not murder! God is concerned with the heart, and the real issue is the hostility that wells up within us and leads progressively to more and more belligerent acts. According to Jesus, even one saying "You fool!" to his brother "shall be in danger of hell fire" (5:22). The truly holy person is not the one who expresses hostility but stops short of murder. The truly holy person is one who *is not hostile!*

But there is even more. Just as the Sixth Commandment as expressed in the Old Testament had both negative [don't murder] and positive [protect others' lives] aspects, so Jesus' explanation of the Sixth Commandment has both negative and positive aspects. As Jesus continued His exposition on the true meaning of Law, He taught, "I say to you, love your enemies, bless those who curse you, do good to those who hate you, and pray for those who spitefully use you and persecute you" (Matt. 5:44).

The holiness called for in the Sixth Commandment has a negative dimension (do not be hostile toward others) and a positive dimension as well (love your enemies)!

Somehow we begin to understand that holiness, true holiness, calls for a radical transformation of both our way of thinking and our heart.

The Desert Landscape

When my family moved to Phoenix, Arizona, one of the great benefits I foresaw was, "No more snow!" And, "No more lawn-mowing!" We decided on desert landscaping.

We'd purchased a home with an extremely large backyard. I expected to have student interns meeting at our home and planned to use the backyard as a place for informal gatherings. So after praying about the timing, we decided to borrow the money necessary to get the yard landscaped. We got a design and a bid from a landscaping firm recommended by the builder, and despite the fact that I had left my midwestern teaching post and had no regular income, we agreed to spend $3,600 on our back and front yards.

The landscaper, whom I'll call Fred, asked for an advance to purchase supplies. I gave it to him. But very little happened in our yard. A dry creekbed that wandered across the yard was dug. That took about two days' work and ten days' wait. Then I was told more money was needed as a down payment on shrubs and for river rock. Again I gave Fred the money. And again, very little happened.

Finally even I, noted for my naivete, became suspicious. I called the nursery. Fred hadn't put any money down. And the amount he'd asked for as a "down payment" was more than enough to purchase all the plants in our design! I was upset and angry. That $3,600 was a lot of money for a person who was unemployed except for income from Christian writing. It didn't help that I felt like a fool for trusting Fred. Those hostile feelings Jesus warned against began to surge.

It was then God brought to mind the verse I quoted above. "Love your enemies. Bless those who curse you. Do good to those who hate you. Pray for those who spitefully use you and persecute you." I got the family together, told them what had happened, read what Jesus said, and we prayed together that God would enable me to love Fred and do him good despite what he had done to us.

A couple of days later I talked with Fred. I told him that I knew what he'd been doing, but that I was willing to fulfill my contract with him. I wouldn't trust him with any more "advances." But I would pay him for each day he worked, and go with him when he bought materials and pay for them myself.

The day after, as we drove together in his pickup truck, he told me his story.

"Larry," he said, "these last two weeks have been rough. My partner pleaded guilty in a suit and forfeited our bond. Then he cleaned out the bank account and left town. Then my wife kicked me out of the house and told me our three kids weren't mine. I was sleeping in my truck with my dog.

"Some folks I was working for said they wouldn't let me finish their jobs, and the suppliers I was using cut off my credit. Then my truck broke down. When I jumped out to see what was wrong, I broke my ankle. I got my truck fixed and my ankle in a cast. Then a couple days later I was driving at night, and the truck broke down again. I hobbled to a phone booth and called a friend to come get me. Then I remembered I didn't tell him where I was, so I almost ran to get back to the truck before he got there. I was so weak that when I tried to pull myself up into the cab, I fell and broke my ankle again.

"But what really got me, I was driving along and happened to turn to a Christian radio station. When I was a kid, I used to sing in a choir. I even sang a solo once in the The Church of the Open Door in Los Angeles. Well, for years I've only listened to country, but that song was so familiar I started to sing along. I opened my mouth, but nothing came out! I tried it again, but I just couldn't sing. And I thought, I guess God has deserted me too.

"Then I came over to your house. You told me you knew what I'd done, but that you'd work with me anyway. And when I went out yesterday, I thought, I guess maybe God hasn't given up on me after all."

A few weeks later Fred walked the aisle of a little church at the base of Moon Mountain and for the first time trusted Christ as his Savior.

You know, there's no way that you or I can keep from feeling hostile when we suffer real or imagined injuries. There's no way we have the capacity to love those who have shown themselves to be our enemies. But as we commit ourselves to live by God's Word, and as we rely completely on the Holy Spirit to do in our hearts what we cannot do, He will work. Our hearts will be changed, and we will be enabled to live the holy life that God calls us to know.

FOR REFLECTION

1. How does the biblical distinction between personal killing and judicial killing or killing in war help clarify thinking about capital punishment?

_____

_____

_____

2. How is the shift of boundaries from action to inner attitude illustrated in the true story of Fred and the desert landscaping?

_____

_____

_____

3. In what relationship do you most need to commit yourself to return love rather than hostility?

_____

Before going on to the next chapter, meditate on this reading on John 15:1–17 from the Personal Growth™ Study Bible.

Abide in Me. The image is powerful even though the words seem unusual. "Abide?" Today we'd probably say "Stay close to Me."

What happens if we stay close to Jesus by obeying His commands? Just as branches draw strength from the vine we draw strength from Him. As His life flows through us the fruit of the Spirit is produced in our personalities (see Galatians 5:22, 23). We bring glory to God and live joy-filled lives.

What happens if we fail to obey? We're disconnected from the flow of that spiritual power we need to produce fruit. Our lives become dry and empty. As far as fruitfulness is concerned—and this is the subject of Christ's analogy—we are as useless as the dried-up vines farmers toss in the fire.

How important it is to stay close to Jesus. How important to do His Word and be filled with the power for holy living that only God can provide.

YOU SHALL NOT COMMIT ADULTERY

*T*he *Star* carried the actress's words in two-inch headlines on the front page. "Affairs made our marriage stronger." Roger smiled bitterly as he watched the young woman avidly reading the article inside.

His wife, Charlene, was back in Britain, living with another man, while he was left with their two little girls in Florida. She'd visited a couple of times. They'd talked about reconciling. But she wasn't ready for a commitment, she said. And when she went back, and he tried to call her flat, the phone rang and rang. Whenever he tried *his* number, she'd usually answer the phone.

It would have been easy to blame Charlene. She blamed him, and that was easy too. When they'd first married, when he'd been on the road for ten days, he'd slept with someone just one night. Conscience-stricken, Roger had confessed to Charlene and begged her forgiveness. That had been a terrible blow to Charlene, and although she said she forgave him, she never forgot.

Later, Roger's adultery became an excuse for Charlene's own affairs. Like the time she'd gone with her sister to their home in Spain, and brought two men they picked up on the airplane with them to spend the vacation. Roger hadn't known then. Later, when he became suspicious of her late-afternoon lunches and discovered she was meeting another man, Charlene had struck out at him. It was his fault. He was the first to do it, and then actually tell her what he'd done! He never thought how that would make *her* feel. Oh, no, all he'd thought about was trying to get the guilt off his conscience. At least she hadn't burdened him with her affairs. And now that he knew, well, he could just blame himself.

With a last bitter look at the headline, Roger got up and left the doctor's office. Affairs hadn't made *his* marriage stronger. They'd left him alone with two young daughters to raise, hurt by his wife's infidelity and evident hostility, yet feeling too guilty himself to deal with what had happened.

We live in a society where the media tend to present sexual promiscuity as the norm. One of the "wholesome" movies we rented recently portrayed an idealistic young woman looking for romance. The only flaw was that while she was searching for the "right" man, she was sleeping with her fiancé! And this was rated as family fare!

The world of the Old Testament had very similar "modern" ideas about sex. *The Expository Dictionary of Bible Words* notes,

> The biblical commitment to sexual purity, which was so integral a part of God's will for Israel, is striking in view of the role of sexuality in the other religions of the time and area. These religions stressed fertility, and their rites often called for sexual orgies to stimulate the gods and goddesses and thus ensure bountiful harvests. Ritual prostitution by men and women was also part of these religions, and the role of the religious prostitute was viewed as honorable, to be accepted by the respectable of society.[1]

The view that any and all sorts of sexual expression are "normal" and acceptable in respectable society is gaining credence in our culture. Even God's prohibition against adultery is treated lightly.

Prudish?

When someone takes a stand against sexual promiscuity today he or she is likely to be considered prudish. But that's a radical misunderstanding of the Bible's attitude toward sex. After all, God is the one who invented sex. He's the one who designed our bodies and gave us those nerve endings that, stimulated, provide the most intense of pleasures. It was God who said to the newly created Adam and Eve in the Garden of Eden, "be fruitful and multiply," and who approved wholeheartedly the joy the first couple found in each other.

God also approves wholeheartedly the joy that a couple today finds in the marital relationship. He even tells the married in 1 Corinthians 7 not to withhold their bodies from each other except for a limited time, and that by mutual agreement. Something special is intended for sexual experience within the bonds of marriage.

A clue as to what that "something special" is can be found in the Old Testament's adaptation of the images of marriage and adultery to symbolize Israel's relationship with the Lord. God is committed to Israel as a husband commits himself to his wife. Israel is to respond with a matching loyalty, and remain true to Him. When Israel turned to idolatry it was an act of spiritual adultery, the breaking of covenant, the violation of a trust (cf. Jer. 3:1–9; Ezek. 23:1–45; Hos. 4).

At the heart of the meaning of marriage is total commitment. Sexual union symbolizes and reaffirms that commitment. Adultery is the violation of the deepest of human trusts; the repudiation of a commitment which, once made, is to be reaffirmed daily by caring for and sharing oneself with one's spouse.

God approves wholeheartedly the joy that a couple finds in the marital relationship.

While the pagan saw sex as the expression of a natural physical desire, the Bible reminds us that God created human beings with a moral and spiritual, as well as physical, nature, and for a far higher purpose than the selfish satisfaction of physical needs and desires.

What's more, all human beings are aware that sex *is* a moral issue. While the rules about what a person may or may not do sexually differ from culture to culture and society to society, there is no society in which any man may have any woman he happens to desire. Every society recognizes that sexual expression must be regulated, and sees regulation as a moral issue.

The Old Testament is very clear on sexual matters, whether incest, rape, homosexuality, prostitution, or adultery. The boundary set in the Seventh Commandment, "You shall not commit adultery," is shown in case law to imply all sorts of sexual expression outside of marriage. If we were to state the boundary, "you shall not commit adultery," in a positive way, it would come out something like this. "You shall reserve sexual intercourse for the one person of the opposite sex to whom you will pledge lifetime loyalty."

Sex is the seal and symbol of commitment. It is not to be twisted into something that it was never intended to be. And it cannot be so twisted without doing great damage to the persons involved.

Jesus' Explanation of the Commandment

In the same Matthew 5 passage where Jesus explained the true meaning of the command not to murder He comments on the Seventh Commandment.

> You have heard that it was said to those of old, *"You shall not commit adultery."* But I say to you that whoever looks at a woman to lust for her has already committed adultery with her in his heart.
>
> *Matthew 5:27, 28*

This reference to the lustful look has troubled many. How can a person *help* looking now and then? Of course, this is Jesus' point! The Pharisees defined holiness in terms of not violating the law. Yet the law was able to regulate only behavior. And behavior isn't our problem! The problem is located in our hearts, where what we see awakens illicit desire.

There is nothing intrinsically wrong or unholy in a beautiful body, whether a woman's or a man's. Any "wrong" is rooted in our response to that body. And whether our response is hidden inside, as lust, or acted out, as adultery, the response is essentially the same.

The Book of Proverbs has much to say about adultery. One of its most fascinating warnings both reflects and helps explain what Jesus is saying.

> Do not lust after her beauty in your heart,
> Nor let her allure you with her eyelids.
> For by means of a harlot
> A man is reduced to a crust of bread.
>
> *Proverbs 6:25, 26*

Sexual promiscuity reduces a human being to a thing to be consumed for one's own gain or pleasure.

Sexuality: In Marriage and in Adultery

When we think about what we've seen so far, we begin to catch a glimpse of what holiness in the sexual arena involves. God provided sex as a gift to enrich the marriage relationship. Sexual intercourse serves as a seal and symbol of a man and a woman's commitment to each other. "Do not commit adultery" calls on me always to be true, in thought, word, and deed, to my spouse.

It is true that sexual faithfulness is essential for building the kind of trust that leads to oneness in marriage. But sexual intercourse can be experienced as this kind of symbol only when I am true to my spouse on every level of my personality. Only when I care for her, encourage her, share with her, express my appreciation for her good qualities, and in every way seek to nurture her growth, will our sexual relationship be as fulfilling as God intended. The commandment not to commit adultery is God's call to me to be completely loyal to my wife on every level of our relationship, not simply on the sexual level.

But Jesus pointed out that the commandment which condemned adultery also condemned the lustful look. While on the one hand the commandment helps me define the nature of a holy relationship with my spouse, it also helps me define a holy relationship with others! Unlike the harlot of Proverbs 6, I am not to turn *any* woman into a thing to be used for gain or pleasure. No woman, no matter how beautiful, is a "thing" for me to use—even in my imagination! No man, no matter how handsome, is to be desired as an object to be used for a woman's selfish pleasure. Even in her imagination!

I must learn to view other persons as God does, as

individuals of worth who are to be valued for themselves. These others with whom we come in contact are to be served, not used, even as Jesus came not to be served but to give Himself as a ransom for many. When I see others through God's eyes, as persons to be loved rather than exploited, then my relationship with them will begin to be holy too. And I will learn what it means to live as Jesus lived in this world.

Roger and Charlene

There is endless pain caused by unfaithfulness in marriage. Roger hurt Charlene deeply. She has struck back at him, and now excuses her continuing adulteries as a payback for her hurt. She doesn't realize that the deepest hurt is that which she causes to herself. Charlene assumes that Roger's violation of her trust is the reason she acts as she does. But if she had sought the grace she needed to forgive, rather than become more and more bitter, Charlene and Roger could have a strong marriage today. Contrary to popular opinion, adultery is not grounds for divorce. Adultery is grounds for forgiveness, as the Book of Hosea shows.

I must learn to view other persons as God does, as individuals of worth.

But now as Charlene goes from one unsatisfying affair to another, her behavior denies the very concept of loyalty and commitment. In her acting out she rejects the loyal love of God, even as she denies the possibility of a human love that is selfless and loyal. Charlene has adopted our society's view of sexuality, and while claiming her sexual "freedom" has lost that which is most precious and irreplaceable.

One boundary that the Seventh Commandment establishes, which we must not cross, is viewing another human being as merely a sex object, someone to be used.

But there is more to the holiness that this commandment enjoins than maintaining a holy attitude toward our spouse and others. From time immemorial people have dressed to attract the opposite sex. But the question we must ask is, When *we* dress to attract, what are we seeking to attract others *to?* What does our dress say to others about us?

Ads in magazines and on TV have typically relied on presenting women as sex objects. Want to sell something? Then make sure there's a shapely, sexy woman in the picture. Today it goes the other way too. One contemporary ad has a couple of girls commenting on the buns and pecs of men that walk by. Another has women in an office running to the window to ogle a construction worker taking a soft-drink break. In every case the ads present women or men as objects of the playful lusts of the opposite sex.

When we dress to attract others *as sex objects,* we cheapen ourselves and our value, and cross a boundary established in the Seventh Commandment. As Peter says, "Do not let your adornment be merely outward—arranging the hair, wearing gold, or putting on fine apparel—rather let it be the hidden person of the heart, with the incorruptible beauty of a gentle and quiet spirit, which is very precious in the sight of God" (1 Pet. 3:3, 4). The Seventh Commandment reminds us that we are far too valuable to present ourselves to others as if we were mere objects for them to use, whether with their eyes or by the act of adultery.

FOR REFLECTION

1. The author suggests the Seventh Commandment establishes a variety of boundaries. What does each of these boundaries imply?

(1) Be totally loyal to your spouse.

_____

(2) Learn to view and treat others as persons of worth and value rather than as mere sex objects.

_____

(3) Learn to present ourselves, by the way we dress and act, as persons of worth and value rather than as mere sex objects.

_____

2. Which of the three boundaries do you have the greatest need to establish right now?

_____

3. The author observed that adultery is grounds for forgiveness, not divorce. To explore the issue of divorce and remarriage further, see his *Remarriage: A Healing Gift from God* (Word).

Before going on to the next chapter, meditate on the following commentary on Proverbs 5:20–35, from the Personal Growth™ Study Bible.

No one believes that committing adultery is morally right. Yet well over fifty percent of Americans have extramarital affairs. "Not right" doesn't seem to matter.

But adultery also isn't smart. The writer of Proverbs notes that adultery, like trafficking with prostitutes, reduces a person "to a crust of bread" (6:26). The point is important. Sex is a sacrament, a gracious means God has given us to enrich and deepen the marriage relationship. But adultery robs rather than enriches. The adulterer, however much he or she may protest, *uses* sexual partners to meet personal needs. Sex outside of marriage is not an act of love, but an act of exploitation.

The writer goes on to spell out implications of our misuses of sex. We can no more help being scarred by adultery than we could help being burned if we held fire to our breast, or walked on hot coals. Our sexuality touches the very essence of who we are. Misuse it, and we injure our essential self.

1. *The Expository Dictionary of Bible Words* (Grand Rapids, MI: Zondervan, 1991), 22.

YOU SHALL NOT STEAL

"So you might know, it was the one time we took Schnapsie with us!"

Beth was telling her best friend, Kerri, about their break-in. "So we take the dog. I just know if we'd left Schnapsie at home, with the size of his bark, there's no way we'd have been robbed. So there goes the TV, the tape deck, even the stainless steel flatware.

"What was worst of all, though, was when we opened the door and saw the mess. Why, they tore everything up. Dumped out all the drawers. Threw all my clothes on the floor. Even pulled everything out of the refrigerator, and dragged it into the hall. I guess they were trying to take it too.

"It makes you feel—you know—violated."

Violated

If we look at the case law in the Old Testament which explores practical implications of the Eighth Commandment, we get the impression that the way stealing violates another person is of major concern.

> If a man steals an ox or a sheep, and slaughters it or sells it, he shall restore five oxen for an ox and four sheep for a sheep.
>
> *Exodus 22:1*

> If the theft is certainly found alive in his hand, whether it is an ox or donkey or sheep, he shall restore double.
>
> *Exodus 22:4*

> If a man causes a field or vineyard to be grazed, and lets loose his animal, and it feeds in another man's field, he shall make restitution from the best of his own field and the best of his own vineyard.
>
> *Exodus 22:5*

These quotes illustrate an important feature of all Old Testament law. Crimes were committed against the victim. In contrast, in our system, crimes are treated as if they were committed against the government. Thus if the person who robbed Beth's house is caught and brought to trial, the indictment will read "John Doe vs. the State of North Carolina." And probably the goods John Doe stole will be kept by the police department as evidence, so Beth and her husband may not regain use of their goods for months. If found guilty, John Doe will be sentenced to prison. But nothing will be done about the sense of violation that Beth feels so intensely. And nothing will be done to repay the couple for their loss, or to restore a sense that it's safe to live in our society.

This isn't the true meaning of Old Testament case law. Old Testament case law is rooted in awareness of the fact that when a person steals another's goods, he has violated that individual and threatened the tranquility of society itself. The first and most important issue is not how to punish the criminal, but how to restore the victim's sense of well-being and the sense for all that society is a safe place in which to live.

The solution in Old Testament law is expressed in the principle of restitution. Because crime is committed against the victim rather than the state, the victim's sense of being violated must be dealt with. At the same time, fear that the society is a dangerous place in which to live must be removed. This is done not by sending the criminal to jail, but by having the criminal make restitution to the victim.

In cases where the original item or animal cannot be recovered, restitution is to be four- or fivefold. In cases where the original item or animal can be recovered, restitution is to be double. In a case where the misappropriation of a person's property is unintentional, restitution is to be equal, with the proviso that restitution must be made "from the best of his own field and the best of his own vineyard," (Ex. 22:5).

When restitution is made, the sense of violation is reduced, and a sense of social harmony is restored. All in the community feel that the right thing has been done, and the strains and tensions created by any criminal acts are reduced. People once again feel safe.

Of course, restoring harmony between the criminal and victim is not the only issue. There's also the need for the criminal to restore his harmony with the Lord. So other passages point out that after making restitution, a person who has stolen must offer sacrifices for sin to the Lord. But the criminal's relationship with God can only be restored after restitution has been made to the victim!

Why Violated?

It's clear that in providing this remedy when someone does cross the Eighth Commandment's boundary a very real sense of violation is involved. But why?

Why is it so important for schoolchildren to wear the kinds of clothing and shoes others wear, and use the same colognes that others use?

Why does Beth feel violated when her home is broken into and her possessions taken?

Why does an older person, almost invalid, alone after the death of a spouse, insist on living at home among the memorabilia of a lifetime?

Why does a person resist a carjacker with a gun and risk being killed?

Why do even young children grip a favorite toy and shout "It's *mine!*" when Mom urges him or her to "share" with a visitor?

The reason goes back to something very basic in human nature. Human beings were shaped by God from the dust of the earth, and then God breathed into them "the breath of life" (Gen. 2:7). We are material *and* spiritual beings. As material beings we live our lives in the physical universe. We depend for our existence on the air we breathe, the water we drink, the food we eat. To a significant extent we define ourselves in our material existence by the things we possess.

If you walk into our garage you'll see on one wall a cluster of fishing poles. Now, there are far more fishing poles there than I can use on any one fishing trip. But I like to think of myself as a flexible fisherman: there are rods to use for grouper or shark fishing, other rods for freshwater bassing, others for hunting redfish or snook, and ultralight rods to use when seeking baitfish, etc. I have an affection for those rods. They're important to me, not for their cash value, but because they are linked closely with my sense of who I am.

I wouldn't be upset if my car were stolen. It can be replaced. But if someone were to take my Wilson Hammer tennis racquet, which I use five days a week, I'd be very upset. I love my tennis racquet; it's closely linked with my identity. And you can take my TVs. But leave my computers alone.

> **G**od provides for restitution, His unique way to restore our sense of wholeness and well-being.

It is simply a fact of human life that we depend on some of our possessions to make possible our existence in this material world, and that other possessions are intimately linked with our sense of personal identity. No one can steal from another without threatening either his or her life, or threatening his or her sense of identity. It's no wonder, then, that we feel violated when someone breaks in and steals. And it's no wonder that God, who is sensitive to our nature, not only commands "do not steal," but also provides for restitution, His unique way to restore our sense of wholeness and well-being.

Bring back the very fishing poles you stole, and I'm comforted. Say, here's the pole I caught my first shark on when we moved to Florida! My, that was an adventure. We were in this thirteen-foot Boston Whaler and something grabbed my bait, leaped four feet into the air, and took off. Thirty minutes later I got it to the boat and saw it was a shark. I didn't know what to do, but I had a salmon net we used in Michigan in the boat. Only half the shark fit in the net, but somehow I got it in the boat. Now what? All I could do was sit on that shark—and not get up. While Sue and Matthew huddled at the not-so-far other end of the boat, I tried pounding on the shark with a hammer. It struggled harder. Desperate, I took a knife and cut away at its throat. Then, for twenty minutes, I sat on the thrashing shark while it bled to death—and while it smashed the trolling motor on the back of my boat to bits.

When we got it home we measured it. It was 5'7" long, and after bleeding still weighed nearly 100 pounds. That was the last time I tried to bring a live five-foot shark into a boat.

But what memories I have as I hold that recovered rod in my hand. Add to it another rod, handed to me by the person who stole, and my sense of violation is gone. But fail to recover that very rod, and it will take at least five more just like it to help me heal.

Oh yes, the boundary, "you shall not steal," is a vital one for human beings who live in the material world.

The Inner Boundaries

It's popular with some to ridicule the notion of private property, and with some contempt to suggest that the truly spiritual or "advanced" individual will adopt some form of Christian or secular communism. They say the notion that we should have private property is "selfish," and an economic system such as capitalism which emphasizes the right to private property corrupts us.

God challenges us to use our possessions in a godly way.

This notion is wrong, for two reasons. First, it ignores the nature of human beings as persons who must live in a material universe, and who to some extent define themselves in terms of possessions. Second, it ignores the implications of the fact that we were created spiritual as well as material beings.

God created us this way. *He intends that our spiritual nature have priority, and determine the way we live our lives in this world!* Material possessions are important to us, and God guards the right of each person to his or her own possessions. Only if we have ownership of material goods will we have the opportunity to choose what to do with them. In giving us the right and freedom to possess private property, God also challenges us to use our possessions in a godly way.

The Old Testament urged those who could afford it to give generously to the less fortunate, and loan them money without charging interest (see Lev. 25:35–37 and especially Deut. 15:7–11).

The New Testament reflects this same attitude. Look, for instance, at the generosity exhibited in the early Jerusalem church.

> Now all who believed were together, and had all things in common, and sold their possessions and goods, and divided them among all, as anyone had need. So continuing daily with one accord in the temple, and breaking bread from house to house, they ate their food with gladness and simplicity of heart.
>
> *Acts 2:44–46*

> Nor was there anyone among them who lacked; for all who were possessors of lands or houses sold them, and brought the proceeds of the things that were sold, and laid them at the apostles' feet; and they distributed to each as anyone had need.
>
> *Acts 4:34, 35*

But isn't this Christian communism? Not at all. It's an expression of spirituality. It's evidence of holiness. For each person freely chose to use his possessions for others, with no external constraints. The Holy Spirit moved these believers to value others more than possessions, and to give generously to meet others' needs.

In 1 Timothy the apostle Paul warns that "the love of money is a root of all *kinds of* evil, for which some have strayed from the faith in their greediness, and pierced themselves through with many sorrows" (6:10). We live in a universe where there will always be a struggle for dominance between material and spiritual motivations. We can choose to love money and, as the thief, use people. Or we can choose to love God and others, and use money in a godly and holy way.

There is nothing wrong with being wealthy. But as Paul says later in this same letter, "Command those who are rich in this present age not to be haughty, nor to trust in uncertain riches but in the living God, who gives us richly all things to enjoy. *Let them* do good, that they may be rich in good works, ready to give, willing to share, storing up for themselves a good foundation for the time to come, that they may lay hold on eternal life" (6:17–19).

The commandment, "you shall not steal," seems so straightforward on the surface. The boundary it establishes seems to be just, "Don't take what doesn't belong to you." But if we look beyond the commandment, and see how Old Testament case law treats the crime of stealing, we see that the Eighth Commandment is saying something profound.

God guards our right to private property because, as individuals who live in a material world, we to some extent take our temporal identity from the things we possess. Even more important, God guards our right to private property because as individuals who are essentially spiritual, having private property creates the chance to choose between living a secular and a holy life.

The daily decisions of those who choose to live a secular life reflect the ultimate value they place on material possessions. And the daily decisions of those who are concerned with holiness—who truly dedicate themselves to God and His values—must surely reflect this commitment too.

FOR REFLECTION

1. Have you ever been the victim of a robbery or theft? How did it make you feel? Why? Was the situation ever resolved so that you felt harmony was again restored?

_____
_____
_____

2. The author suggests two reasons why the Bible affirms the right of private property. Which of the two seems most important to you?

    a) To some extent we define ourselves by what we possess.

    _____

    b) Possession of private property gives us the opportunity to choose to live a secular or godly life. Private property is essential to holiness.

    _____

3. How holy do you feel your life is, measured by the way you use your money?

_____

_____

_____

Before going on to the next chapter, meditate on the following comment on 2 Corinthians 8:9–15 from the Personal Growth™ Study Bible.

New Testament giving is intensely personal. We Christians are not commanded to give a certain percentage as a duty. The New Testament epistles make it very clear that giving is to be voluntary (9:7). What characterizes New Testament giving is that it is a personal response to need.

We may not know the individuals who need our help. The Corinthians didn't know those whose needs Paul shared with them. Corinthian hearts were simply touched by his report of privation. Love then moved them to give.

In the church giving is not a redistribution of wealth. Paul doesn't believe in freeloading (cf. 2 Thess. 3:10). But the apostle encourages us to consider the fact that some may need our help now to survive, understanding that at another time we may be the ones in need.

Before we give, let's measure the real needs of others against what God has graciously given us, and respond generously in love.

YOU SHALL NOT BEAR FALSE WITNESS

*I*t's one of the most familiar phrases on TV, repeated again and again on courtroom shows. "Do you swear to tell the truth, the whole truth, and nothing but the truth, so help you?"

It's an appropriate phrase to think of as we begin our look at the Ninth Commandment for, as case law clearly shows, the boundary set by the Ninth Commandment applies directly to criminal and civil legal cases. Yet this commandment, as do all the others, suggests other boundaries that the individual who seeks to live a holy life will want to establish, and live within.

"I think Carol's the one," Esther whispered to her husband as they sat in church. Luther just shrugged and turned his head away.

Esther leaned closer. "She had the chance. She was at the church all the time. And she lost weight. That's a dead giveaway. The only time a woman can lose weight is if she's having an affair or about to divorce her husband. It's just *got* to be Carol."

The congregation had been shocked three weeks earlier when their pastor resigned and confessed to committing adultery. The elders, looking very solemn, had assured the congregation that their pastor was repentant and was submitting to the counseling and restoration program the denomination required. But since then everyone had heard that the woman or women involved had refused to confess and seek forgiveness, as the pastor had. Still, soon it was common knowledge that the adulteress was someone within the congregation. Now rumors flew, as everyone speculated who the "other woman" might be.

Esther, even more sure of her reasoning now that she'd expressed her thoughts to her husband, turned around and motioned to Debbie. When Debbie leaned closer, Esther whispered loudly, "It's got to be Carol . . . ."

In middle school our thirteen-year-old had a standing to maintain. She was proud of her reputation as "the first one to know."

She was the first to know who held hands with whom. She was the first to know who had asked whom out. She was the first to know who dumped whom. She was the first to know what Karen had said about Tracy, or what Tony thought of Melissa. It gave her a real sense of importance when someone after school came up to share the latest, and she could say, "Oh, I knew *that* at lunch time."

Gossiping about others can do serious harm.

I don't think there was anything wrong in what our young teen was doing. At that age, while sports are important to many of the boys, what the girls think and wear and do, and who the boys like, takes center stage for many girls. Friends and their relationships dominate some young girls' thinking and talk. But hopefully that consuming interest in the concerns of others won't characterize our daughter when she grows up and matures. At least not to the extent that talking about others becomes the be-all and end-all of her life. Not to the extent that, as Esther, she either has to know, or speculate about, the faults and flaws and sins of others.

The truth is, it's dangerous to talk about others. Even when we're sure of our facts, gossiping about others can do serious harm. And, if we go back and take a look at the boundary set by the Ninth Commandment, speculation is unquestionably wrong.

The Obligation to Speak Out

The Old Testament legal system was very different from our own. We've seen one difference, in that system's emphasis on restitution rather than punishment. Another difference is in the fact that Old Testament law presupposes no national or even local police force. All God's people were expected to take personal responsibility to live by His law. And, in cases where civil or criminal disputes arose, all were responsible to aid a resolution that also accorded to God's law. Such issues were to be dealt with locally, by local elders who knew the character and reputation of those involved, and who knew the witnesses. Only when a case was too difficult for local elders to decide was the matter to be taken to the central court, composed of a panel of priests. This group was then responsible for determining the facts in difficult cases, and then issuing a judgment based on God's law.

Several things were necessary if the biblical justice system was to work. It was necessary to have as judges godly local elders who could not be bribed (Ex. 23:8) and who would not show partiality. It was also necessary for any in the community who had knowledge of a matter in dispute, or knowledge of law-breaking, to come forward and testify to what they knew (cf. Lev. 5:1).

Thus in the Old Testament legal justice system it was essential that witnesses testify, and that they testify truthfully to that about which they had personal knowledge. Several items of case law that illustrate the Ninth Commandment make clear how critical this was, and yet how vulnerable the society was to false witness.

> You shall not circulate a false report. Do not put your hand with the wicked to be an unrighteous witness.
> You shall not follow a crowd to do evil, nor shall you testify in a dispute so as to turn aside after many to pervert *justice*.
> You shall not show partiality to a poor man in his dispute.
> You shall not pervert the judgment of your poor in his dispute.
> Keep yourself from a false matter; do not kill the innocent and righteous. For I will not justify the wicked.
> And you shall take no bribe, for a bribe blinds the discerning and perverts the words of the righteous.
> *Exodus 23:1–3, 6–8*

One of the things we note from these injunctions is how easily a person can be influenced to spread a rumor or testify falsely. It may be that you're simply following the crowd. If everyone believes Carol did it, you assume they're right. Rather than speak only that which you know from personal knowledge, you speak about Carol as if your words convey the truth. Or maybe you feel sympathy for a poor person, or one who suffered a terrible injury. So you shade your testimony to favor him or her against an insurance company. After all, the insurance company can afford it. Or perhaps you hope to gain from being on the side of the wealthy in a dispute, and so "pervert the judgment of your poor." Perhaps there is something else you hope to gain by shading your testimony, or keeping a rumor alive. The many warnings against false witness in case law, and the situations case law deals with, make it clear that we human beings can find both "legitimate" and selfish reasons for failing to tell the truth, the whole truth, and nothing but the truth. How vulnerable individuals and society are to becoming victims of false testimony!

In fact, Old Testament law sets up further requirements to guard against the false witness.

> One witness shall not rise against a man concerning any iniquity or any sin that he commits; by the mouth of two or three witnesses the matter shall be established. If a false witness rises against any man to testify against him of wrongdoing, then both men in the controversy shall stand before the LORD, before the priests and the judges who serve in those days. And the judges shall make a careful inquiry, and indeed, *if* the witness *is* a false witness, who has testified falsely against his brother, then you shall do to him as he thought to have done to his brother; so you shall put away the evil from among you. And those who remain shall hear and fear, and hereafter they shall not again commit such evil among you.
>
> *Deuteronomy 19:15–20*

It was to take two or more witnesses, each speaking from personal knowledge, to even have a case heard! And, if the judges determined that a witness testified falsely, that false witness was to receive the penalty that the person he accused would have suffered if he actually had committed the act.

The Nature of False Witness

What, exactly, is "false witness"? In Exodus 19:16 the Hebrew word for "false" is *seqer,* a term that describes "groundless" words. Groundless words are deceiving because they have no basis in fact. Thus a false witness is anyone who accuses another person of something which has no basis in reality.

In Deuteronomy 5:20, where the Ninth Commandment is repeated, a synonym is used. Here "false" is *saw'*, a word usually translated "empty" or "vain." The words of a false witness are empty, for he or she presents as real something which is insubstantial and unreal.

Whatever the intent of the false witness, whether to harm another person, make oneself look and feel important, go along with the crowd, or simply repeat a rumor, false witness involves charging another person with *anything* without substantial grounds and a basis in fact.

A witness must have personal and direct knowledge of that to which he testifies. Without direct and personal knowledge, he or she must keep silent, and cannot speak out.

It's obvious that Esther has stepped over this boundary in speaking of Carol. She has suspicions. She may even be right! But for Esther to voice her suspicions is to accuse a sister of something about which she has no direct, personal knowledge. Her charge, insubstantial and without grounding in facts, marks her as a false witness.

All our gossip shares something of this character and is condemned in the New Testament (see Rom. 1:29; 2 Cor. 12:20; 1 Tim. 5:13).

In fact, the New Testament's attitude toward gossip helps us understand the implied boundaries established by the Ninth Commandment. The behavioral boundary is obvious. Tell the truth about others in court. Don't speak about them without personal knowledge that any accusation you may make is true. But as Jesus taught in Matthew 5, the behavioral boundary set by Old Testament commandments testifies to a deeper, truer *intent* expressed in them. The person who seeks to live a holy life today looks *within* the commandments, as he or she seeks to understand its source in God's deepest desire for us.

As we look more deeply at the Ninth Commandment, we see that its heart and intent is clearly expressed in the New Testament. This is particularly clear in Romans 14. There Paul urges believers to welcome each other, especially the weak in the faith, "but not to disputes over doubtful things" (14:1).

What Paul is speaking of here as a doubtful thing is any matter of personal conviction on which the Scripture fails to speak clearly. Adultery and murder are not "doubtful things." These are behaviors which God clearly identifies as sin, and says "you shall not." But what about all those things on which Christians differ, and the Bible is silent?

What about whether or not to eat meat (14:2, 3)? What about what day to keep, and how to keep it (14:6)? What about all those myriad matters which are essentially personal? Should a woman wear makeup? Should a man hunt deer? Should a person pray for healing and refuse to see a doctor? Should a person go into a bar to meet a non-Christian friend? Should a Christian give a tithe, or more, or less? Who should you marry? When should you move? What job should you take? Is it "Christian" to see a psychiatrist? Can a Christian teenager be a cheerleader in high school? Should she take another course of chemotherapy, or hope the cancer will have a remission on its own? Should a person who doesn't speak in tongues be an elder? Should a congregation welcome a person who does speak in tongues?

The list is endless. And it should be. While the behavioral boundaries established by the Ten Commandments and other clear "do's" and "don'ts" of Scripture are to be maintained within the Christian community, in all other areas we are to extend to each other the freedom to live *without being judged by each other.*

This is the point made in Romans 14. "Who are you to judge another's servant" (v. 4)? And, "to this end Christ died and rose and lived again, that He might be Lord of both the dead and the living" (v. 9).

Jesus is Lord.

Jesus Christ alone is qualified to judge the choices we make regarding "doubtful things."

> The person who seeks to live a holy life must look *within* the commandments to understand the source of God's deep desire for us.

The Ninth Commandment teaches us not to bear false witness by speaking groundless, empty words against a brother. When Esther gossips about Carol she is judging her, groundlessly accusing her if not of the act of adultery at least of being the kind of person who might well commit adultery. This is clear. But when we criticize a brother or sister for the way he or she exercises freedom in Christ, we are doing the same thing! Whatever is said by the crowd, whatever our personal convictions on the matter may be, we have no right to judge another of Jesus' servants.

Understanding this helps us understand and choose to live within the boundaries the Ninth Commandment implies. Holiness calls on us to renounce and reject our tendency to judge. When we consciously reject our tendency to judge a brother or sister's motives or spirituality, we establish a boundary in our hearts which enables us to live holy lives.

FOR REFLECTION

1. The church is to discipline Christians who continually violate the clear moral commands of Scripture (see 1 Cor. 5:1–8). What is the difference between judging Christians who sin and judging others' exercise of their Christian freedom?

_____

_____

_____

2. What are you most likely to be judged about by other Christians? Can you remember times others have spoken critically of you?

_____

_____

_____

3. What are you most likely to judge others for? Can you remember times you've spoken critically of them?

_____

_____

_____

Before going on to the next chapter, meditate on the following insight into Romans 14 from the Personal Growth™ *Study Bible.*

Ever been with Christians who are so convinced that they shouldn't do something—like eat meat—that they insist you can't either? Here are some principles governing personal convictions about things on which the Bible is silent. See if you can find each in Romans 14.

• Welcome into fellowship believers whose convictions differ from yours.

• Don't look down on or condemn those who differ. Don't pressure them to accept your view.

• Two Christians may have opposite convictions—and both be right!

• Jesus is Lord. Don't take Christ's place in another's life by judging him or trying to impose your convictions. Give others the freedom to be accountable to the Lord.

• Don't flaunt your freedom to do something that is against another's convictions.

• Be more concerned with each other's spiritual welfare than with asserting your right to act on your convictions.

• And, in matters of conviction, don't act against your conscience, even if intellectually you're convinced it's all right.

YOU SHALL NOT COVET

"My nose is just too big," Melissa said judiciously, rotating the mirror to examine the offending feature from every angle.

"No doubt about it," she pronounced.

"Big."

Like most her age, Melissa couldn't help feeling self-conscious about her body. She knew that Casey was upset because her breasts hadn't developed yet, but Casey was cute and slim and everyone liked her. And Shannon was overdeveloped, and terribly embarrassed by her big bust. But Shannon was so energetic and fun. No, Melissa thought, again judiciously. She was the only one of her friends whose life was going to be ruined because she looked like a freak.

"If only my nose looked more like Kristi's," she thought. "Then I might have a chance."

With a deep sigh she put down her mirror and stood up, ready to face another dreadful day.

If you read books on the characteristics of young teens, you'll meet lots of kids like Melissa. Most feel self-conscious and embarrassed about some part of their physical makeup. They're too tall or too small. They develop too early or too late. Their noses or ears are too big or too little. They're too fat or too thin.

In my day, it was my hair. In those long-ago days before hair styling, my multitude of crowns made my hair stick out in every direction. This wasn't helped by the fact that my dad used a bowl when he cut my hair with a pair of clippers that caught and pulled hairs unmercifully. I credit my hair with one of my early nicknames—Bushman—and with the fact that all through my high school years I remained dateless. No girl in my class wanted to be seen with a guy who looked as if he'd just stuck his finger in an electric socket.

Thankfully, those painful days passed. I've reached the point where I can live comfortably with my hair. And I'm told by some that since it's turned silver, I even look slightly distinguished. When I brush and comb it.

For some people, however, the painful days never seem to pass. As adults they still wish for Kristi's nose, or Johnny's muscles, or Terry's six-foot frame, or Deborah's figure. They truly feel that they and their life would be different if only they looked a little different.

I suspect that this is the reason for much cosmetic surgery. Here's Melissa's chance! She can have that nose that looks like Kristi's. And then Melissa will be a different person! And life will be all sparkling and fresh and new.

The Tenth Commandment

When we read the Tenth Commandment we're struck by the fact that it's radically different from the others. Except for the first, each of the other nine sets a clear behavioral boundary. Don't worship idols. Don't take God's name in vain. Don't work on the Sabbath. Honor your parents. Don't murder. Don't commit adultery. Don't steal. Don't bear false witness. These are laws whose violation we have some chance of measuring. We can see a person's idol. We can examine the body after a murder is committed. The person who bears false witness utters words we can hear and evaluate.

But the Tenth Commandment says,

> You shall not covet your neighbor's house, you shall not covet your neighbor's wife, nor his male servant, nor his female servant, nor his ox, nor his donkey, nor anything that is your neighbor's.
>
> *Exodus 20:17*

Whatever else we say about this commandment, it's clear that coveting is not an observable behavior. I can covet someone's house without ever taking possession of it. I can covet someone's wife without committing adultery with her. I can covet his ox without stealing it. Coveting is something that happens *inside of me!*

The Hebrew word translated "covet" is *hamad*. It means to desire, or to take pleasure in. Other words constructed on this root are translated "pleasant" and "desirable," so it's clear that desire is not wrong in itself.

It's perfectly right for me to take pleasure in my own house. There's nothing wrong in finding my own wife desirable. In fact, I *should* desire and take pleasure in the good things that God has provided.

There are, of course, things that I should not desire because they are intrinsically wrong. I'm not to desire a prostitute (Prov. 6:25), or the gold that overlays a pagan idol (Deut. 7:25). But covetousness is different. Covetousness isn't a desire for evil. It's a desire for something good run riot, not because the object of my desire is intrinsically wrong, but because the object of my desire is something—anything—that belongs to my neighbor.

If my heart is free of covetousness, I have learned to understand myself in relationship to God.

It is at this point that we begin to see the deepest meaning of the Tenth Commandment, and understand its link to the First Commandment. If my heart is free of covetousness, *I have learned to understand myself in relationship to God.*

The Lesson of Spiritual Gifts

One of the most encouraging New Testament teachings is found in 1 Corinthians 12:7. There we're told that every believer is given at least one spiritual gift by the Holy Spirit. This spiritual gift enables us to minister to others; to have a positive, nurturing impact on their lives.

The passage makes it clear that there is a wide variety of spiritual gifts. It even names many of them. But the passage also makes two extremely significant points. Paul writes that "one and the same Spirit works all these things, distributing to each one individually *as He wills*" (12:11; italics mine). God is the One who chooses which gifts we will receive. He is the One who sovereignly bestows. In essence, the Holy Spirit is the One who gives us our identity and role within the body of Christ.

The second extremely significant point the passage makes is found in Paul's illustration, which casts believers as parts of a human body. Paul is well aware that we human beings tend to honor some parts of our body more than others. We think [rightly] that our head is more important than our hand, and

vastly more important than a big toe! But, Paul says, this
simply isn't true in the Body of Christ. In fact, "those members
of the body which seem to be weaker are necessary" (12:22).
Each one of us is a vital part of the Body of Christ, whatever
role we may play in it or whatever spiritual gift God may have
chosen to give to us.

This teaching helps us put the commandment "do not
covet" in perspective. The person who sits in the pew, and
thinks "I wish I could sing like him," is coveting another's gift.
The person who studies for the ministry, and thinks "I wish I
could speak like that person," is coveting another's gift. And
coveting is so unnecessary! For we each have our own gift, our
own ministry, our own role in the Body of Christ. Even more,
we are exactly the person that God wants us to be!

Melissa's Nose

When Melissa looks at Kristi and covets her nose, Melissa
is acting appropriately for a young teen. She's growing up and,
hopefully, will become more comfortable with herself as she
matures.

But when you or I look at another person and covet her
looks, or his possessions, or her gifts and abilities, we are not
acting appropriately. We're not acting appropriately because we
fail to consider that God has created and shaped us to be
ourselves—not someone else! We have not yet realized that
holiness involves *living for and serving God as the persons we are,
in the circumstances in which He has placed us.*

In a fascinating passage in the New Testament, Paul
encourages slaves to be the best slaves they can be. Don't
constantly think about how life would be if you were free, he
writes. Take advantage of the circumstances in which you find
yourself to serve God and others now (see 1 Cor. 7:17–24; Col.
3:22—4:1).

Paul doesn't mean that if a slave has a chance to purchase
his freedom he should not take it. What Paul is saying is that
whether one is the slave or one is the master, that person has
God-given opportunities to serve the Lord and other people. In
fact, it is being the slave or being the master that gives each his
unique opportunities to serve.

I do not have to be a different person to be significant in God's scheme of things. I do not have to have my neighbor's house or job to have opportunities to serve God. In fact, God has shaped me and my circumstances in order that this unique person who "I" am might serve Him faithfully *as* I am. God has shaped me and my circumstances in order that this unique person who "I" am might express His love and compassion to those I come in contact with.

If my circumstances were different—if I could speak like that preacher, if I did live in that expensive house across town, even if my hair hadn't stuck out every which way as a teen—I would be a different person than God intended. And I would miss opportunities to minister to others that God has planned for me from the beginning.

 God has shaped me and my circumstances in order that "I" might serve Him faithfully *as* I am.

Here we see the link between the First and the Tenth Commandments, the two commandments which do not establish clear external, behavioral boundaries. The First Commandment says I am to have no other gods "before" the Lord. I am to purify my understanding of who God is until I know Him as He has revealed Himself in Scripture. Loving. Wise. Just. And, of course, Lord—the One who is Always Present With Us, always active and sovereign in our lives.

If I truly know and honor God as He is, stripped of the masks with which my imagination disguises Him, then I must acknowledge that He has shaped me and my circumstances for His own good and loving purposes. And I simply cannot covet anything my brother has. Instead, I must delight in fulfilling the purposes that God had in mind in creating "me" me!

What a joy we find in being content with our looks and our lives. What release we experience when we realize that there is no reason for us to envy others or wish that we were different than we are. What joy we can find in the freedom Jesus gives to accept and be ourselves. What fulfillment we can find in concentrating our energies not on coveting, but in being

the best we can be, and on grasping every opportunity that
God gives us to do His will.

Holiness Now

We began this book with an intent to better understand
holiness and learn what it means for us to live holy lives today.
We saw in Isaiah's experience of God as Holy, Holy, Holy that
we must begin our search for holiness by acknowledging
that we are sinners, accepting God's gift of forgiveness, and
committing ourselves to serve Him.

We then sketched the difference between the Old
Testament's concept of ritual holiness, and the dynamic inner
holiness that Jesus explained, a holiness which is both hidden
and revealed in Old Testament commands. This launched us on
a study of the Ten Commandments themselves, to better define
the external boundary set by each, but more importantly to
discern the inner boundaries that we are to establish in order to
maintain healthy and holy relationships with God, with others,
and within ourselves. The chart on pages 103 and 104 sums up
our discoveries, and reviews the guidelines for holy living the
Ten Commandments contain.

What is exciting about our study is the fact that while you
and I have no ability to live a holy life, God has given us His
Holy Spirit. And how significant this is! Have you ever noticed
that in nearly every reference in the New Testament, the
descriptive word "Holy" precedes "Spirit"? Have you ever
wondered why?

Why don't we find the same pattern in references to God
the Father? Only one time, in the prayer recorded in John 17,
does Jesus refer to God as "Holy Father." When speaking of
Jesus the New Testament doesn't identify Him as "Holy Jesus,"
or "Holy Christ," or "Holy Lord." There is no doubt that the
Father and the Son *are* holy. But it is only the Spirit who is
regularly identified as the "Holy Spirit."

Why? Because it is the mission of the Holy Spirit to work
in your life and mine and *enable us to live Holy lives!* The holy
life we yearn for and cannot live on our own strength is exactly
the life that God's Holy Spirit has come to produce in us. As
we face the challenges raised in the Ten Commandments, and

understand the boundaries God calls us to maintain in our hearts and relationships with others, let us face them with confidence and joy. The Holy Spirit is with us.

The Holy Spirit *will* enable us to live holy lives.

FOR REFLECTION

Check over this summary of the implications of each of the Ten Commandments for holiness today. Invite the Holy Spirit to take charge of your life and enable you to grow in holiness day by day.

THE TEN COMMANDMENTS

No.	The Commandment	External Boundary for Israel	Holiness Lesson for Us Today
1	No other gods before Me (Ex. 20:3).	Reject pagan concepts of God.	Develop accurate God concept from Scripture.
2	Do not make graven images (Ex. 20:4).	Do not worship or rely on idols.	Let no material object stand for God or serve as evidence of His favor/disfavor.
3	Do not take God's name in vain (Ex. 20:7).	Do not claim to speak for God when you do not.	Remember at all times and in every circumstance that God is real and present.
4	Keep the Sabbath Day (Ex. 20:8).	Do no work on the Sabbath	Set aside time away from the cares of this life to focus attention on the Lord.
5	Honor father and mother (Ex. 20:12).	Support parents in their old age.	View parents with love, understanding, compassion, and forgiveness.

THE TEN COMMANDMENTS—*Cont'd*

No.	The Commandment	External Boundary for Israel	Holiness Lesson for Us Today
6	You shall not murder (Ex. 20:13).	Do not kill another for personal reasons.	Identify hostile feelings as sin. Show love to enemies.
7	You shall not commit adultery (Ex. 20:14).	Reserve sexual intercourse for marriage.	Be loyal to spouse in word and deed. View all other members of the opposite sex as persons of value rather than as sex objects.
8	You shall not steal (Ex. 20:15).	Do not take any possessions of others.	Use private property in a godly way, guided by our commitment to God's values.
9	You shall not bear false witness (Ex. 20:16).	Tell only the truth in court cases.	Do not criticize or judge another's motives or spirituality in any matters left to individual conscience.
10	You shall not covet (Ex. 20:17).	Do not desire what belongs to others.	Accept yourself and circumstances as God's gifts, and use every opportunity to serve.

TEACHING PLAN

What is Personal Growth?

To live healthy and happy lives we need to be growing in three important dimensions. We need to grow in our personal relationship with the Lord. We need to grow in our intimate relationships with others. And we need to grow within, developing a strength of character that will enable us to meet life's challenges successfully.

Personal Growth™ Study Guide Books

Personal Growth™ **Study Guide** books are intended to help believers grow in their relationship with God, their relationship with one another, and to strengthen Christian character. They teach foundation principles found in the Word of God, and help believers apply them to daily life. These are essentially inspirational and practical books that major on personal application of God's Word.

This makes them ideal for use in a Bible study group, whether the group meets Sunday mornings as a Sunday school class, or for in-home Bible study. The Teaching Plan is designed to show a leader in any study group how to draw on the book and the group members' own personal experiences to have a truly significant learning experience.

Leading a Study Group

Some study groups have assigned teachers. Other study groups rotate leadership among members from week to week. Whatever approach you use in your group, the Teaching Plan is workable and easy to follow. One of the most important things to remember is that the leader of a study group is as much an *encourager* and *motivator* as an instructor. Because each member of the group will have the book you are studying, it isn't as necessary for the leader to teach content. The book provides the content, although the leader should be prepared each week to review key concepts for anyone who has not done the reading. As encourager and motivator, the leader will seek active participation

by group members and encourage the kind of sharing that
motivates members to put God's Word into practice.

A Simplified Teaching Plan

The Teaching Plan for each chapter is simple and easy to
follow. The plan features:

Starter Activities:	These serve to open the hearts of group members to the truth explored. Starter activities usually involve participation.
Focus Activities:	These sharpen group members' understanding of the issue being explored and/or of a vital Personal Growth biblical principle.
Application Activities:	These help group members see how Personal Growth principles apply to life in general and their lives in particular.
LifeSharing Activities:	These help group members motivate and encourage one another, pray for and support one another.

God bless you as you teach.

CHAPTER 1: GOOD NEWS FOR IMPERFECT PEOPLE

Materials Needed:
Chalkboard, chalk
Holiness Checklist from pages 4–5 for each member
Books, Bibles

Starter Activity:
1. Introduce yourself.
2. Explain Personal Growth and the role of *Personal
Growth™ Study Guide* books (see above, or Preface).
3. Ask each member to introduce himself or herself and tell
why he or she elected to be involved in this study of Holiness.

Focus Activities:
1. Have each group member think of the "holiest" person
he or she has ever known.

2. Go around the group, telling about the person each member identified and explaining what about this person seems "holy."

3. Read the brief story told by Harry Ironside, as reported at the beginning of this chapter. Discuss: What do your group members think this story illustrates about holiness? (Let each express his or her opinion freely. There is no "right answer" to this question.)

4. Distribute the "Holiness Checklist." Discuss each of the four options in A through E together.

Application Activities:

1. Read the verses on holiness from 1 Peter. Point out that whatever holiness is, God has called us to a life of holiness. Express your conviction that as you study together the Lord will be at work, developing this quality in each one.

2. Distribute books and assign Chapters One and Two for next week.

CHAPTER 2: HOLY, HOLY, HOLY

Materials Needed:
Chalkboard, chalk
Paper, pens
Books, Bibles

Starter Activities:

1. Review what the author tells about Bob on page 1 of Chapter One, and under "Revisiting Bob" on page 12 of Chapter Two. Ask, Which of us can identify with Bob? Can we understand how Bob felt?

2. Discuss: What kind of persons would be most likely to argue that "holiness" is a bigger pain than gain to Christians? Why would they take that position?

Focus Activities:

1. The author suggests that we need to understand essential truths about God if we are to grasp the meaning of holiness for believers. Invite members to share anything significant they learned about God from Chapter Two. (Note: Avoid correcting "wrong" ideas at this point.)

2. On the chalkboard write the author's understanding of the three dimensions of God's holiness:

> Holy—Lord, I am overwhelmed by a sense of my sinfulness.
> Holy—Lord, You forgive and cleanse me.
> Holy—Lord, from now on I set myself apart to You.

3. Look together at Isaiah 6:1–9. Trace how Isaiah's experience with God fits into this three-dimensional pattern of holiness.

Application Activities:

1. Write on the chalkboard the three-column analysis that appears in item 1 of **For Reflection.** Ask each member to determine which of the three "holy's" of Isaiah 6 best describes where he or she is today.

2. Discuss: What is the most important reason we would want to move from a one-dimensional experience of holiness to a two-dimensional? From a two-dimensional experience to a three-dimensional experience?

3. Read the note on Exodus 4:10–12 quoted from the *Personal Growth™ Study Bible.* Share: How would this perspective help us move from a two- to a three-dimensional experience of holiness?

Lifesharing Activities:

1. Ask each person to write a single paragraph describing personal goals he or she would like to reach through this study of holiness.

2. Have the group break into pairs or threesomes. Encourage each who is willing to read the paragraph he or she has just written. Then pray for each of the pairs or threesomes.

3. Assign Chapter Three for next week.

CHAPTER 3: INSIDE OUT

Materials Needed:
Chalkboard, chalk
Books, Bibles

Starter Activities:

1. Just for fun, list some of the stated or implied "do's" and "don'ts" that many in your congregation(s) assume distinguish "good" and "poor" Christians.

2. Share: Have any of you felt frustrated by the existence of this kind of list? In what way(s)?

Focus Activities:

1. Give your group members a quiz to check on their understanding of the important concepts introduced in this chapter. Be sure to check your own understanding by rereading the chapter before class.

   a. What did Jesus mean when He said He came to "fulfill" the Law? [Explain its true meaning.]
   b. Old Testament law set up "external boundaries." [Law governed behavior, actions.]
   c. How in Matthew 5 did Jesus shift these boundaries? [He showed the implications of God's law for inner thoughts and attitudes.]
   d. What inner boundary is indicated by "don't murder"? [Anger and hostility are wrong.]
   e. What inner boundary is indicated by "don't commit adultery"? [Value others, don't view or use them as "things."]

2. If the quiz shows that many group members have not grasped the essential contribution of this chapter, work through the Matthew 5 verses "you have heard . . . but I say" to illustrate the shift from external to internal boundaries.

Application Activities:

1. Read aloud the following from the text. "How shocked Jesus' listeners must have been. They supposed that if they did not murder, did not commit adultery, and kept any vows they made, that they were holy. And then Jesus started talking about anger, lust, and integrity! Why, Jesus' words challenged the very foundations of their ideas about holiness."

2. How do Jesus' words challenge *our* ideas of what it means to be holy? How would group members change any ideas they have previously had about holiness in view of what Jesus taught?

LifeSharing Activities:

1. Share experiences: Has it been easier for you to act in a loving way or feel a deep love for another? Why, or why not?

2. God intends to make us holy by transforming us from within. Invite each group member to read and meditate for sixty seconds or so on the note on Jeremiah 31:31–34.

3. Conclude with encouragement: God is committed to transforming us. He can and will enable us to live the holy life to which we are called. Pray that each member will be open to God's work through this study.

4. Assign Chapter Four for next week.

CHAPTER 4: NO OTHER GODS

Materials Needed:
Chalkboard, chalk
Books, Bibles

Starter Activities:

Review the direction the study is now taking. Old Testament holiness involved living within *external* boundaries defined by God's Law. Jesus showed that the true boundaries that define holiness are *internal*. Thus we are now going to look at each of the Ten Commandments, to see what internal boundaries each suggests for our relationships with God and others.

Also remind the group that while three-dimensional holiness leads to a knowledge of our sinfulness, confession and forgiveness, and then commitment, we must rely on the Holy Spirit to enable us to live holy lives.

Focus Activities:

1. Ask group members to recall the common notions of "god" mentioned in the chapter. [List them on the chalkboard as they are recalled: compulsive, grandfather, fault-finding.] See what other common notions about God your group can describe, and "name." List these on the chalkboard too.

2. This chapter analyzes the notion of a "compulsive" god in view of Jesus' teachings on God as Father. Look together at Matthew 6:5–14 and 6:25–34. What in these verses corrects the impression Joanna had of a god who answered every prayer—if she met seven "conditions"?

Application Activities:

1. The author says that the first inner boundary we must establish in our adventure toward holiness is one that keeps out false notions of who God is.

Look at the notions about God listed at the beginning of your session. Let group members suggest Scriptures which correct false notions about who God is that are listed there.

2. Discuss: The Bible is the only revelation by God of Himself in our language. What does this imply about how we are to test notions we and others may have about God? How would we go about testing an idea about what God is like?

LifeSharing Activities:

1. Have group members jot down ideas about God which have affected their lives, positively or negatively.

2. Ask members to share the ideas each wrote down and tell something of the impact each idea has had on his or her life.

3. Ask group members to repeat a brief affirmation of faith based on the First Commandment:

> God wants me to know Him as He is.
> God has revealed His true self in the Bible.

4. Close in prayer, thanking God for being Himself, and asking the Lord to reveal more of His beauty and love as you study together.

5. Assign Chapter Five for next week.

CHAPTER 5: NO LIKENESS OF ANYTHING

Materials Needed:
Chalkboard, chalk
Books, Bibles

Starter Activities:

1. Go around the group and ask each member how circumstances have at times affected his or her feelings about God and His love.

2. Discuss: When are Christians most likely to see material blessings as signs of God's favor? [When they are poor or struggling? When they're sick? Etc.]

Focus Activities:

1. Read the Second Commandment. Ask: What boundaries did the commandment establish for Old Testament believers? Discuss: Why do you suppose the desire to "see" gods or goddesses was so strong in people then?

2. The author gives illustrations that suggest people today also have a strong desire to "see" God in material things. Have group members recall the illustrations.

3. Ask your group members to work together to state the *inner boundary* implied in the Second Commandment. Write their ideas and revisions on the chalkboard, until all are satisfied with the statement.

4. The author says "the Second Commandment had become an inner boundary for Paul that kept his heart content." What does the author mean, and what evidence is there in Scripture that this is true?

LifeSharing Activities:

1. Read the author's statement: "When we do the same, and set the Second Commandment as a boundary within our hearts, we realize that we 'see' no more or less of God in the good things that befall us than in the tragedies. God is no more present with us in wealth than in poverty, in sickness than in health."

2. Invite members to share personal experiences of a sense of God's presence in truly difficult or tragic times.

3. Ask your members to affirm aloud with you:

"God loves me completely.
God loves us always."

4. Let volunteers thank God for a love that we experience, but that no material thing can prove or disprove.

5. Assign Chapter Six for next week.

CHAPTER 6: TAKING GOD'S NAME IN VAIN

Materials Needed:
Chalkboard, chalk
Books, Bibles
3" x 5" card for each member

Starter Activities:

1. Ask, "Have you ever felt uncomfortable because people around you swore and cursed using Jesus' name? If so, what did you do?"

2. Did the author's observation that the commandment against taking God's name in vain isn't addressed to nonbelievers make you feel better about what you did or didn't do? Why?

Focus Activities:

1. Review the meaning of God's name, the LORD, as explained from Exodus 6. The central reality of that revelation is that God is One who is Present With Us Always.

2. Review the incident of Hananiah's false prophecy uttered in God's name. Discuss: How did that violate the *external boundary* the Third Commandment established for Old Testament believers?

3. Work together as a group to write a definition of the *internal boundary* that the Third Commandment establishes for Christians today.

Application Activities:

1. Brainstorm: How and when are believers today most likely to take God's name in vain?

2. You ended each of the first two sessions with an affirmation of faith based on the commandment you studied.

> 1. God wants me to know Him as He is.
>   God has revealed His true self in the Bible.
> 2. "God loves me completely.
>   God loves us always."

This week, repeat together an affirmation based on the Third Commandment:

> 3. "God is present with me.
>   God can act for me now."

3. Distribute three-by-five-inch cards. Ask each member to record these affirmations on one side of the card, leaving room for another affirmation to be added next week. Encourage them to carry the "commandment card" with them and refer to it now and then during the week.

LifeSharing Activities:

1. Ask for opinions. What difference would it make if every Christian were constantly aware that God is not only present with us but also able to act in any situation?

2. Have members read and consider for two minutes the note on Psalm 94 taken from the *Personal Growth™ Study Bible.*

3. Ask volunteers to close in prayer, praising God for who He is for us.

4. Assign Chapter Seven for next week.

CHAPTER 7: REMEMBER THE SABBATH

Materials Needed:
Chalkboard, chalk
Books, Bibles

Starter Activities:

1. Discuss: What activities weren't allowed on Sunday when you were growing up? What positive things were done in your family to make Sunday special?

2. OPTION. Would it be a good thing if no one in your house were allowed to watch TV on Sundays? With what might you replace it?

Focus Activities:

1. Discuss: What struck you most in the description the author gives of the way the Jews more and more closely defined the external boundary established by the Fourth Commandment: "do no work"? Is making rules about what we can or can't do on Sunday the best way to make sure we honor the Lord? Why, or why not?

2. The author believes the association of the Sabbath with God's great acts and relationship with His people is important for understanding the inner boundary implied. What conclusion does he draw [end of chapter, page 55]?

3. Work together to develop a group definition of the inner boundary the Fourth Commandment establishes.

Application Activities:

1. Discuss: Which "cares of this world" crowd our lives so much we're too tired or simply don't seem to have time for God?

2. Have each individual decide when he or she could find just thirty minutes to set aside "work" and focus on the Lord. Let each then tell what time slot would be best for him or her.

3. Have group members add the following affirmation to their "commandment cards," and repeat all four affirmations in unison.

> 4. "God invites my attention.
>   I will set aside time for Him."

4. Challenge group members to set aside that thirty-minute period they identified each day this week to focus on the Lord in prayer, Bible reading, or meditation. Jesus said that the Sabbath was made for man, not God (Mark 2:27). The greatest benefit in taking time to focus on the Lord is ours, not His.

5. Assign Chapter Eight for next week.

CHAPTER 8: HONOR PARENTS

Materials Needed:
Chalkboard, chalk
Books, Bible

Starter Activities:
1. Invite those who set aside time to maintain the Sabbath's inner boundary last week to share their experience. Also ask those who carried and referred to their commandment cards to tell of any times when the reminder was helpful to them.

2. If Richard, Fran, and Sis were to pick two words to describe their relationships with parents when growing up, what words do you think they would have chosen? Write on the left side of the chalkboard.

3. Ask each member to select two words that best represent his or her relationship with parents when growing up. Ask each to share the words selected, and tell a little about his or her parents.

Focus Activities:
1. Read Mark 7:10–13. Discuss: What does this confrontation tell us about the weakness of treating biblical commands as establishing only external boundaries? [NOTE: You may need to review the author's discussion of vows and

the "practical" approach of the rabbis to help group members see how easily external boundaries can be manipulated.]

2. Discuss: How does the inner attitude of Sis demonstrate the establishment of a Fifth-Commandment "inner boundary" in her heart? How do Richard and Fran cross that inner boundary?

LifeSharing Activities:

1. Ask group members to write down two words that best describe their present relationship with parents, if parents are living. Write these on the left side of the chalkboard. Discuss: What does a comparison of the list tell us about the way we're keeping the Fifth Commandment?

2. Remind your group that bitterness is "natural" when a child has parents like those described in this chapter. But God through Christ can and will work to write His Word on our hearts.

3. Work together to develop a definition of the inner boundary suggested by the Fifth Commandment.

4. Pray that God will work in each member's heart to establish that boundary and free us from bitterness or anger toward our mothers and fathers.

5. Assign Chapter Nine for next week. Encourage group members to continue the thirty-minute discipline this coming week.

CHAPTER 9: YOU SHALL NOT MURDER

Materials Needed:
Chalkboard, chalk
Books, Bibles

Starter Activities:

1. Discuss: When you first read the talk-show host's monologue on the execution, how did you feel? Did you agree or disagree? Why?

2. Poll: Invite group members to vote by a show of hands. If you were on a jury that found a person guilty of murder, could you recommend the death penalty? Yes, or no?

Focus Activities:

1. Ask for volunteers to explain the distinction the author says Hebrew makes between "personal killing" and killing in war or by judicial decree.

2. Ask for volunteers to explain "case law," and cite case laws that illustrate both negative and positive external boundaries that grow out the command "You shall not murder."

3. Look together at Matthew 5:21, 22. How does Jesus reach his conclusion about the true meaning of the Sixth Commandment? [NOTE: By tracing personal killing back to its roots in hostility and anger. This is where we are to draw the inner boundary that we must not pass if we are to live holy lives.]

Application Activity:

Work together to define the inner boundary, both positively and negatively that is implicit in the Sixth Commandment. Write the group definition on the chalkboard.

LifeSharing Activities:

1. The author tells a true story about his "desert landscape" experience with this commandment. Ask, Have you had any similar experiences you can share with us?

2. Have group members read the note on John 15:1–17 from the *Personal Growth™ Study Bible.* Jesus alone is the source of that new life which enables us to live within the Law's inner boundaries and live holy lives.

3. Urge group members to continue to set aside time to be with the Lord. Holiness is possible only as we stay close to Him, so that His life flows through us.

4. Assign Chapter Ten for next week. *NOTE: If your group is enjoying this* Personal Growth™ *Study Guide book, now is a good time to pick out a follow-up text for another thirteen weeks together. And if you've profited from the* Personal Growth™ *Study Bible notes at the end of each chapter in this book, some in your group will want to order a* Personal Growth™ Study Bible. *Call your local Christian bookstore.*

CHAPTER 10: YOU SHALL NOT COMMIT ADULTERY

Materials Needed:
Chalkboard, chalk
Books, Bibles

Starter Activities:

1. Invite group members to share what's happening in those private thirty-minute devotional times. What impact are they having on the rest of the day?

2. Discuss: What impact does the media's presentation of sexuality have on marriages today?

Focus Activities:

1. The author restates the external boundary established by the Seventh Commandment as "You shall reserve sexual intercourse for the one person of the opposite sex to whom you will pledge lifetime loyalty." Does this seem to provide sufficient guidance in sexual matters? Why, or why not?

2. Look together at Matthew 5:27, 28. What inner boundaries do you believe Jesus' restatement implies? [List suggestions.]

Application Activities:

1. The author suggests three areas in which the Seventh Commandment implies inner boundaries that the person striving for holiness is to maintain. Let group members choose one of the three areas and meet as teams to discuss what their area implies for Christians.

        a. Total loyalty to spouse.
        b. View and treat members of the opposite sex as persons of worth and value rather than sex objects.
        c. Present ourselves, by the way we dress and act, as persons of worth and value rather than sex objects.

2. After ten minutes, re-gather, and have teams report their ideas.

LifeSharing Activities:

1. Discuss: What wrong ideas about sexuality have been the hardest for you to get rid of? What was the source of these ideas in the first place?

2. Commit: Share one thing you plan to do this coming week that honors the Seventh Commandment's inner boundaries.

3. Set aside a few minutes to ask God to bring each member's attitude toward himself or herself and the opposite sex into full harmony with this vital commandment.

4. Assign Chapter Eleven for next week.

CHAPTER 11: YOU SHALL NOT STEAL

Materials Needed:
Chalkboard, chalk
Books, Bibles

Starter Activities:
1. Ask each group member to think of two things he or she would most hate to have stolen. Then list each person's name on the chalkboard, along with the two things he or she selected.
2. Have one person sit on a chair in the center of the group. Have group members suggest what the two items he or she chose tell about his or her feelings about who he or she really is. Repeat with other group members.

Focus Activities:
1. The author says that personal possessions are protected in God's law, and sees two basic reasons why this is important. Ask the group to recall the two reasons, and explain why each is important. [Possessions help us define who we are in our life in this world; possessions give us the opportunity to make decisions guided by our spiritual rather than material nature.]
2. Discuss: How important is the Old Testament's reliance on restitution rather than punishment for theft, and why?
3. Look together at Acts 2:44–46 and 4:34, 35. Discuss: What evidence is there in the text that this is *not* "Christian communism," and why is this important?

Application Activities:
1. Have group members read the note on 2 Corinthians 8:9–15, from the *Personal Growth™ Study Bible*. Discuss: Why would the Law's requirement of giving ten percent fall short of encouraging true holiness? How does this passage further develop the positive implication of the "do not steal" inner boundary?
2. Predict: Would it make any difference if the way all Christians used material resources was controlled by our spiritual nature and commitments? If so, what differences might we expect?
3. Suggest that sometime this coming week group members review their spending and budgeting in view of the inner boundaries established by this commandment.

4. Remind the group again that it is God who enables us to live out the true meaning of God's commandments. That's why it's so vital to maintain that thirty-minute-a-day time with Him.

5. Assign Chapter Twelve for next week.

CHAPTER 12: YOU SHALL NOT BEAR FALSE WITNESS

Materials Needed:
Chalkboard, chalk
Books, Bible

Starter Activity:
Share: Have you ever been the victim of gossip? What happened, and how did it affect you?

Focus Activities:
1. Look together at Exodus 23:1–3, 6–8. How do these case law rulings illustrate boundaries implied by the Ninth Commandment? What are some of the pressures identified here that might have led a person to offer false testimony?

2. What insights do the Hebrew words for "false" provide that help us define the inner boundary implicit in the commandment against false witness? [See "The Nature of False Witness," p. 92.]

3. Look together at Romans 14. The author suggests that this passage defines the inner boundary implied in the commandment. How can we help feeling judgmental when another Christian does something that violates our convictions? [NOTE: The church is to affirm God's judgment that an act is sin when a brother or sister repeatedly violates a clear teaching of God's Word. The subject of Romans 14 is "doubtful things"— e.g., things not unmistakably labeled as sin in Scripture.]

LifeSharing Activities:
1. The author says, "When we consciously reject our tendency to judge a brother or sister's motives or spirituality, we establish a boundary in our hearts which enables us to live holy lives."

Share: What is most likely to arouse a judgmental attitude in your heart?

2. Pray for each other that God will replace any judgmental attitude with His own spontaneous love and gift of

freedom for each believer to be responsible to Jesus only in areas of personal conviction.

3. Assign Chapter Thirteen for next week. Remind each person to bring his or her "commandment card" to group.

CHAPTER 13: YOU SHALL NOT COVET

Materials Needed:
Chalkboard, chalk
Books, Bible
Extra three-by-five-inch cards

Starter Activities:

1. Share: Go around the group and once again ask each person to share one thing about themselves that they truly like: one thing that is good about being "me."

2. Discuss: Was it easier saying something positive about ourselves this time than before? Why, or why not?

Focus Activities:

1. To reserve time for summing up this study, cover the key points made in this chapter in a brief lecture. Be sure to show the link between the First and Tenth Commandments, the only two which do not have clear behavioral boundaries for God's Old Testament people.

2. Afterward, ask if anyone has any questions or issues raised in the chapter that he or she would like to discuss further.

Application Activities:

1. Have students turn to the chart on pages 103–104. Earlier they summarized the first four commandments as "affirmations of faith." Now, together, develop a series of brief "commitments" that express the meaning of the last six for believers today. Each commitment can take the form,

> "I will . . . ."

Each should be as brief as possible, but adequately sum up what the commandment implies.

2. When your group has agreed on the six commitment statements, have them record these commitments on the back of their three-by-five-inch "commandment cards." [Have extra

cards available if any members have misplaced or failed to bring their own.]

LifeSharing Activities:

    1. Share: Encourage group members to share any special work of God in their lives that has taken place during your study together.

    2. Conclude with a time of praise, not only for the Lord Himself, but for each other as God has shaped each of you for His good purposes.